A Shadow of Me

The Oklahoma City Bombing and How It Changed My Life

Jennifer Mangini

Quill Hawk Publishing

Cover designed by Ava Wood, Fins and Feathers Designs

ISBN: 978-1-965142-11-0 (Paperback)
ISBN: 978-1-965142-12-7 (Hardback)
LCCN: 2024917017

Content Warning: Material contains swearing, discussions of death, depression, drugs alcohol, homelessness, PTSD, suicide ideation, and other topics that may trigger readers.

CONTENTS

To my brother Tony.

As children we had more adventures together than either of us probably remember. As adults we have carried a bond that stayed strong even when I was so lost, and you had to be the one showing tough love.

Thank you for being my brother.

When joining the U.S. Army, new recruits take the **Oath of Enlistment**. Here's how it goes:

"I, [name], do solemnly swear (or affirm) that I will support and defend the Constitution of the United States against all enemies, foreign and domestic; that I will bear true faith and allegiance to the same; and that I will obey the orders of the President of the United States and the orders of the officers appointed over me, according to regulations and the Uniform Code of Military Justice. So help me God."

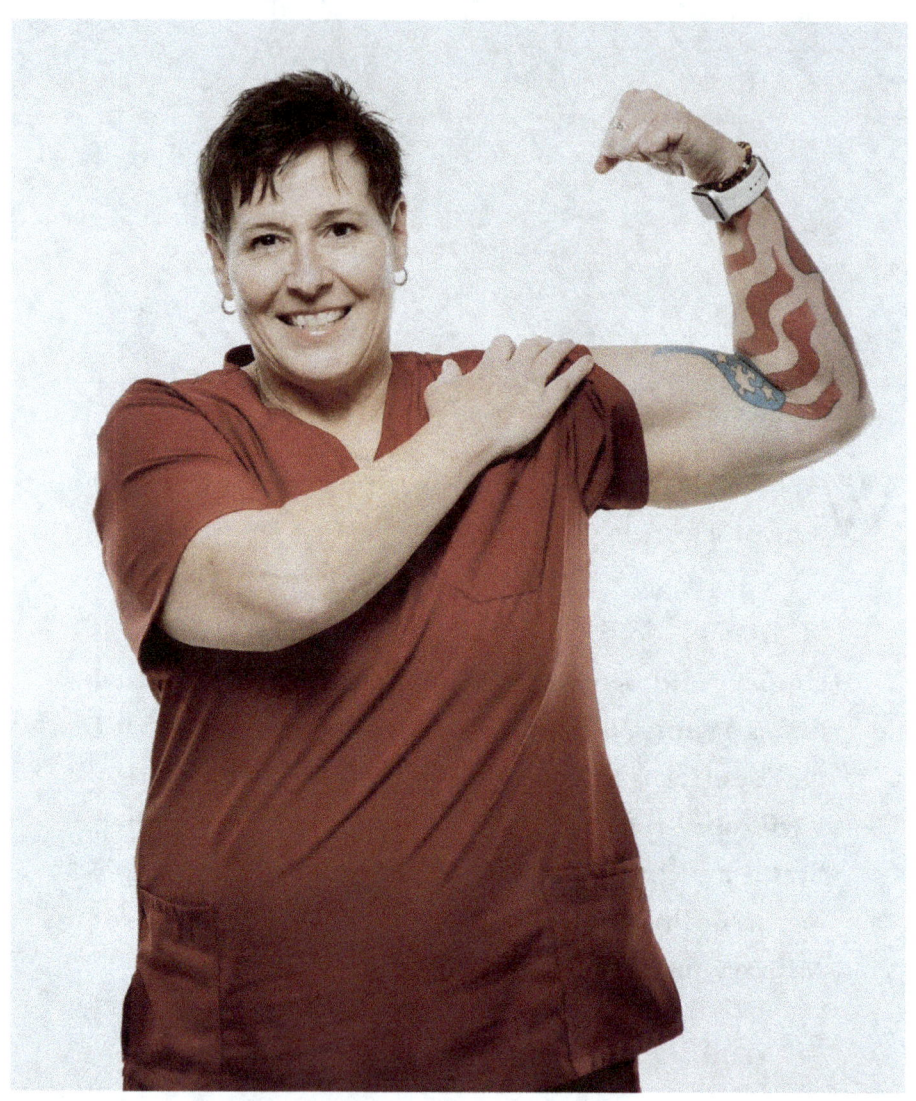

PROLOGUE

9:01am. April 19,1995

A bomb of more than 4,800 lbs of fertilizer and fuel in the back of the yellow Ryder rental truck ignited, causing a massive explosion to rip through the nine levels of the Alfred P. Murrah Federal building. The blast was so strong that it completely tore away the building's north side. The gaping crater showed a tangled heap of concrete, broken, bent steel beams, and debris. The Ryder truck no longer existed, and the cars and vehicles around the area were burning. Black thick smoke billowed and there was a grey smoke rising, like a dragon, to mark the building's destruction.

This was a retaliation strike towards the American government by Timothy McVeigh and Terry Nichols. They were responsible for the death of 168 people and hundreds were wounded when they bombed the Oklahoma City's Murrah Federal Building. This was in response to the incident on April 19,1993, when the FBI raided the Branch Davidian compound in Waco, resulting in the death of 76 cult members, including 25 children.

Oklahoma Alfred P. Murrah Service Medal (Oklahoma Bombing)

INTRODUCTION

I think trying to author this book is a bit like fishing-in the middle of a storm. Hopefully somewhere warm, but not too hot. Okay, scratch that, because now I tend to be hot-blooded (not because I am mad, but because I am trying to keep my over 40's hormones in check!) so I am picturing ice fishing right now...wearing shorts, sitting on some seriously thick warm blanket, and wearing some Gortex jacket and gloves, boots, and a cute beanie.

Of course, the storm is inside my head and there are no literal fish, except Goldfish crackers which are the best snack of all time, except for maybe Doritos. Okay, now that I had to get a snack, and my dogs had to have their snack, because, of course, they couldn't let me snack alone. They're like large furry alarms, going off the moment I crunch the first cracker or even open the box.

Inside my head there are so many things I want to write, to say, stories that I think would really be impactful and hopefully help a person whose story is not where they want it to be... and they see that there can be hope.

Some stories or ideas are funny and bring you to the point where you laugh lying on the couch and wipe your tears with your sleeve because it is a laugh-cry and so cleansing to the soul.

This life and this world have so much that is not fun, however, and this book will capture both the laughter and the struggles. Because isn't that balance what we try to achieve in life? is that balance?

Back to my fishing analogy. I pick out a story or thought that I want to share and I grab it, (or cast my line to it in my imagined fishing expedition). and Maybe I get a nibble or straight up bite, and then I get a text, or my dog barks, and it is gone. Lost to the abyss or at least somewhere in this head of mine that can still recite classmates from eighth grade or my home phone number and address when I was a child. Yet it is a struggle to know what I ate yesterday or where I parked when I got to work.

When I do get those serious bites and can stay focused long enough to reel in, it is usually not a normal little thing but more like that sea creature from "Finding Nemo" or "Creature from the Black Lagoon." It is a bit of a hurry up and wait game, (which is awesome because I learned that early on in the Army) but a great catch once the memories latch on. Then, you, the reader, and I can feast on the story.

I am trying to convey that it is hard to pick the right story or moment and the correct words, meanwhile my tinnitus is humming like a high-pitched Christmas carol stuck on play since last January. My self-talk critiques every single word, (Are you sure that is what you want to say? Or do you want people to know you did That?!?) but my heart and my gut say tell it all. Hold nothing back. This is my story to tell.

The original title of my book was I Scratched My Name Off the Wall of Hell: The OKC Bombing & How It Changed My Life, but I thought, I do not want to turn people off or deter them from even considering picking up the book to read the back cover and scrolling down to see what this book is about.

This is too important of a story to be so off-putting just by the words on the cover. This is a story that I hope can give someone who thinks there is no way they can ever live a 'normal' life, be able to afford rent, have a bed inside somewhere safe, have a job, or be able to look at themselves and like what they see in the mirror. But I am getting ahead of myself so let me just tell you this:

I like the title because I feel like in so many ways, I was trapped in this dark and horrible place of addiction, that matrix or fine line that is so blurred but still linked to our universe that humans in both can see each other. Once someone goes to that reality, they just can never find the way back.

When someone goes to a place and they want to make their mark but do not want to ever come back, they will leave something or leave graffiti either way. It can be a memento or something they care about, or simply, their name. There are two ways I look at this. I could have traversed the grotesque halls of hell and broken a bone to scratch my name within its marred, gross black walls, or I could have found my name on the list of people who were scheduled to come and then—with whatever I could find, a bone, a glass pipe, a needle, or damn shovel—carve a deep line through my name. I believe there is a heaven and there is a hell, but I also think there are parts of hell on earth. They are places where a person loses their soul, where they wander like zombies, empty and devoid of living. Their heart beats an empty, hollow beat. It is not brains they seek, but life, their life.

Maybe they are not physical locations, like where you could see mile markers along the highway. (220 miles to hell, and last gas!) Maybe they are somewhere in between. I honestly do not know.

What I do know is the life I have lived. I hope you see the humor in my words, maybe you do not, but this is my story about what I have been through and how I came out alive. It doesn't really fall into a specific genre; it's like a conversation with a friend and also some self-help-ish-ness. It is a bit of a memoir which, like me, does not fit in a box. Please grab a cuppa whatever you're in the mood for and open to chapter one.

To Begin

My name is Jenn Mangini (Man-jee-nee by the way) and I joined the United States Army on 20 January 1991, through the DEPS (Delayed Entry Program). My basic training course took place in Ft. Leonard Wood, Missouri, and I was to report on 20 August 1991. This allowed me to finish the general courses I was taking at the local community college, which meant that I got to join as a Private First Class! This was going to put me somewhere on the military totem pole, not the very bottom rung of the ladder, and I was going to be a combat medic.

Visions of fighting on the front lines danced through my head while I pretended to listen to my professors. The funny thing with day dreaming is there is no physical feeling, no discomfort or pain, just thoughts of grandeur while imagining running up a hill to protect a fellow soldier from incoming gunfire.

This also allowed me a few months to prepare for the physical challenge of being a soldier, and I remember waking up to my alarm clock with a new purpose. I rose at dawn-ish, eager to hit the gym and push my body to new limits. My 5 '8, 146 lb frame was working hard (I thought) to be in shape, and since I had never really focused on doing much physical training before that, I was stoked when I was able to do thirteen "real" pushups! Those thirteen "real" pushups may seem insignificant to some, but for me, they represented a newfound strength and determination. I was going to leave my family home and fly to St. Louis. From there... Well, I just knew this was going to be quite an adventure! I felt a mix of excitement and anxiety as my departure date approached. I packed my bags with all the essentials I believed a future soldier would need (or at least what was on the list the recruiter gave me) and then I meticulously boxed up and correctly labeled all my childhood belongings.

Just kidding. I left my bedroom with a small backpack on my back and did not look back. Of course, I heard about how much I left behind when my dad packed up my room and had to roll up quite a few movie posters (Outsiders, The Lost Boys, The Breakfast Club) a few years later. Sorry, not sorry!

BASIC TRAINING

August in Ft Leonard Wood, MO was HOT! I was totally not prepared for the humidity and heat of the Midwest. It is like breathing without air. Exhausting. The quickest way to get air was to pass out and just lay down, although I was determined not to do that.

We were in formation and getting yelled at for... well, just being there. I felt something on my mid back. I was standing at attention so I could not freak out on the outside, but inside—TOTALLY FREAKING OUT—until I felt it again. (Is something crawling on me? How much trouble would I be in if I just screamed and ripped off my shirt? Wait, that felt more like a drip. Ohh!) I suddenly realized it was a drop of sweat dripping down the small of my back. Seriously.

I found myself in the predicament of wanting to crack up and, of course, could not, because remember, I was in formation. My sweat-soaked clothes clung uncomfortably to my body as I marched in formation with my new sisters in green. You know those moments in time that where you know you will remember for the rest of your life, and you almost feel time slowing to a snail crawl? Here is one of mine.

We were the last all-female basic training company at Ft Leonard Wood, Charlie-4-10. You would have thought—well, I thought—that they would be celebratory about the end of an era. Oh, no, no, no. Nothing of the sort, more like using us as the proving point that women were badass and could do more. Our drill sergeants pushed us harder than ever before, determined to make us the best soldiers we could be, and show us off as an example of female strength and resilience.

It was day one of basic training. We had all gotten our standard-issue BDU's (battle dress uniform: camouflage top with camouflage cargo pants, camouflage hat called a cover, stiff black leather boots, tan t-shirt, white undergarments, and black socks. We marched out of the reception hall and loaded onto the large cattle trucks, with no seating. The driver took corners like it was a NASCAR Sunday Race and then suddenly slammed on the brakes. As we tried to pull ourselves apart, the huge trailer gate opened and a voice boomed, "GO, GO, GO!"

We literally fell out of the cattle truck, unladylike and very ungraciously, like spilled popcorn, and quickly ran to the formation area. The sun was beating down. There was barely a breeze. It was kind of a pretty day, not that I noticed at the moment, because the drill sergeants continued barking commands at us as we fumbled awkwardly in front of them, our duffel bag strapped to our backs, stuffed full and padlocked with shiny new locks. As we were loudly instructed to stand in two long lines on the utility sidewalk, which laid in front of the three large brick buildings, I noticed some of the women were almost shorter than their duffel bags.

I should have been paying actual attention, because as I was mentally complimenting myself of my 5 '8 height and awesome stature, almost towering over my new Army green duffle bag, what I failed to notice was everyone else starting to unlock their new shiny locks.

So let me break in and tell you something about myself. When I get rushed, nervous, anxious, or yelled at, I forget everything there is to forget—my name, your name, my mate's name, mom's name, important phone numbers, passwords, and padlock combinations... (Okay, back to the story.)

"Remove your lock, empty your bag completely onto the pavement in front of you, and hold your bag up in the air."

Sounds easy enough... all up and down the two lines, empty duffels were being held up in the air.

Meanwhile, I am sweating, my fingers are rolling the combination wheels, and my body is tightening up like a corkscrew. And then... EVERYONE is done. Except ME.

I am now a disoriented mess, my mind swirling with chaos, and my body frozen in uncertainty. I had to be dreaming; there was no way I actually joined the UNITED STATES ARM—

"What the hell?" The drill sergeant screamed. "What is your name? How do you even say Mangini and why are you holding all my new recruits up?"

His name was Drill Sergeant Green and he was incredibly angry, loud, and almost on top of me. One more note about drill sergeants—they tend to work in packs. Here came the other ones, like hungry hyenas ready to pounce.

Somehow, by the grace of God, my lock opened, and I could not get my duffel emptied fast enough. It was too late - this very "typical drill-sergeant-looking" drill sergeant made eye contact with me. He memorized me like a predator sizing up its prey. As his eyes bore into mine, I quickly held my now-empty new duffel bag above my head, my heart pounding in my chest as I braced myself for what I knew was going to be an unleashing of this newfound authority over me.

This was the day I learned how to really do pushups. Pushups could be—and would be—done as slowly or as quickly as he could count. Also, (and this was illuminating) I was the one who got to demonstrate the "halfway and hold" position. (Basically, you push up,-straighten your arms, and then bend your arms at the elbows approximately halfway, where no part of your body is touching the ground except boot tips and hands). I did way more than thirteen before I was allowed to stand up.

There was such diversity around me. There were women who were talented runners, unlike me, and women from eastern and southern states with cool, drawling accents, like Rachel Knight, Sherrie Saunders, Martinez, and Monica Neil, to name a few. There were some who were the first females in their family to join the services, and there were some who were looking for the best way out of the small town or large city they felt trapped in. Wherever we had all come from, we started seeing each other as new extensions of ourselves and started learning about true sisterhood.

One of the coolest things we did in basic training was throw a real hand grenade from a very safe platform out into a large rock quarry. I was so excited!! After hours of hearing how we were going to do everything EXACTLY as instructed, and enduring grueling, slow training of squatting, pausing, pulling pin, standing, and finally launching the grenade (like you were throwing a baseball in the World Series), it was time to practice!

"And duck!" Drill Sergeant Green screamed.

Duck, as in take cover. As in not watching. AS IN not watching the explosion.

What? Are you freaking kidding me? I had been dreaming of blowing shit up with hand grenades ever since my brother and I were kids playing in the creek behind our house. I was so excited when I finally got the chance to do it. I was shaking with excitement and anticipation. I could not wait to blow shit up! Yes. I was disappointed with not being able to watch but, seriously, where is the fun in that? Yes, I know we were in basic training for the United States Army. This was not supposed to be fun. I was determined to throw the farthest and then be completely safe and duck. Which I did. I ducked... for a tiny little second. Then I stood up. Why? Maybe because I have been known to live by my own rules, or maybe I was being defiant. I have no idea, but I can now tell you it was not the smartest decision I ever made. The blast of the grenade in the distance was loud, but I actually do not think I saw anything blow up because as soon as I was upright, I was knocked off my feet by at least two amazingly fast, exceptionally large men in thick, protective gear. I guess that was what it felt like to be tackled by defensive linemen... and incredibly angry ones! The whole platoon got yelled at while I, of course, did more pushups than any human ever should (in my opinion of course).

I grew up like many others playing Army. Running with branches like a rifle trying to get the bad guy, getting muddy running through the shallow creek that lined our property, laughing with my brother and dreaming of being a soldier.

So, when I joined the Army and went on my first BIVOUAC (which is really just a cool, fun sounding military word for sleeping and camping—minus a fire—without a real tent, sleeping bag, toothbrush, or pillow). I realized there was a lot more than just running around being loud, laughing and teasing my brother and sometimes super cool cousin Jerry. First of all, being loud was frowned on, as well as laughing. Also, M-16s are heavier than a little oak branch, and sleeping outside is not really an awesome thing.

Weeks of marching. We could not just walk to the barracks, we marched. Wanna go to church? March. Hungry? More marching. We would do 20-mile road marches with full rucksacks and M16s. Sometimes I was granted the opportunity to carry the M60, because I was tall! (Note: just because someone is tall does not automatically make them stronger, except in my case, but I digress.)

I remember marching hot, tired, silent, just boot in front of boot, seeing the dust from the step, the little gnats flying around. Once, while marching, I lulled myself into falling asleep. Yes, you read that correctly. My body simply stopped. I did not fall or sit down. I just stopped and stood there, swaying slightly, fairly sure my eyes were open, but no movement.

The soldier behind me loudly whispered. "Mangini! Hey, why did you stop! Psssst."

Here is one of those moments that I think God must have a comedy channel and just wants to get a good laugh because before my brain registered what she was saying, one of the drill sergeants of course heard her. Suddenly, I woke up face to face with this irritated drill sergeant, who of course yelled a lot, and then of course, I was doing pushups. (I may not remember the total number but I guarantee it was more than thirteen!)

Speaking of pushups—I was the one people lined up to watch do pushups and situps. And, I would run extra miles just to encourage my buddies who hated running. I even had a drill sergeant who taught me how to do one arm pushups and "dropped" with me the day of graduation to do twenty.

So, after being shoved around (more verbal than literal), breaking my nose (first broken bone- and a great story but not for this book), getting yelled at (a lot!), and being pushed outside so far out of my comfort zone that I forgot where my comfort zone was, I graduated a few months later with a sense of pride that was unlike anything I had ever felt. I was a soldier. A real GI Jane... before the movie!

My class had just completed AIT (Advanced Individual Training) in San Antonio, Texas. The future looked great. We were ready for our first duty stations. Excitement filled the air as we packed up our belongings, prepared to scatter across the country to serve and protect. I had dreams of making a difference, of being a part of something bigger than myself.

"PFC Mangini!" (That stands for Private First Class.)"You are going to Fort Sill." The voice barked—because a drill sergeant never just speaks.

"Wait, what? Ft. Sill, Oklahoma? Where is that?-Besides the obvious, Oklahoma, I mean, where is that? And WHY ME?!"

Everyone lined up around me had duty stations that sounded great... Hawaii, Alaska, Germany... But Oklahoma?

So, it was with a confused and heavy heart that I got on the bus to Oklahoma.. just kidding, but I wonder what would have happened if I had been stationed in Hawaii?

Winter 1992 I arrived at my new home in one of the coldest ice storms they had seen in years. The only real wintry weather I had ever experienced was going to Tahoe as a teenager, and that had included actually wearing jeans (not shorts), a hand-me -down "warm" coat, and a lot of peppermint schnapps! I can expertly say that was nothing like living in an ice-covered midwestern state.

That first winter was miserable. There were days the only time I would be warm was in my nice, toasty shower. Not even my bed felt like I was able to be totally unthawed! I also learned a valuable lesson the first week I was in my duty station. While we were in Basic and AIT, I had worn no jewelry, but I started wearing a simple chain my mom gave me. I had taken it off when I went to take a shower. It was a communal shower, and when I came back to where I had laid it with my clothes, it was gone. I might look all bad ass and soldiery, but I was still a pretty naïve young lady.

If you have ever been in the Army (or any branch of military) you know that the term "military grade" does not always mean the best money can buy. Our everyday uniform was named "BDU" or "battle dress uniform" and came in two styles: summer and winter. Winter style was a little thicker and had an extra button fly patch of material to keep certain areas a tiny bit warmer. As you have probably guessed, the summer was a thinner material. We were required to keep our uniforms crisp and neat so I would have mine dry-cleaned weekly. Summers would be so starched that I would literally peel the pant legs apart to put them on! "Winters" material was anti-starch. It did not matter what starch, or if I ironed, they would take a wrinkle like a grape in the sun. I loved the look of my crisp, clean creases running up my legs and across my shirt, so I would wear the "summers" almost all year! The only times I would wear "winters" would be when it was really cold and there was not any kind of inspection or official business going on (so, almost never).

Once, I saw a small water tower spring a leak and as the water sprayed out, it froze, creating a waterfall of frozen spray down the side. It must have been a pretty big deal because the Ft. Sill Post newspaper featured a picture on the front page! This California native was so cold! I never imagined that I would experience such harsh winters when I first moved to Oklahoma. This was the worst cold snap they had had in years, the old guys would say. Ice storms were frequent, and the streets were covered in a thick layer of ice, only you could not see it. Black ice... needless to say, I stayed inside any time I had a choice!

That being said, I fell into Army life quickly and easily. One of the first things I learned was that drinking was the thing to do when not on duty.

Bored? Drink. Happy? Drink. Sad? Drink.

Are you seeing a trend? A pony keg a night was just another Tuesday, and the 6:10 am PT run off the hangover was the typical Monday through Friday. Who taught me that? My First Sergeant.

Jennifer Mangini (right) with dear friend Monica Neil in 1991

THE DAY

My active-duty enlistment was complete. The next phase of my army time was to be a weekend warrior while attending community college and finding a job.

It was early spring 1995. I had gotten an overnight job stocking shelves at Herbs IGA grocery in Lawton, Oklahoma. I had just completed my in-processing into the Oklahoma Army National Guard and was enrolled in general classes at the local college.

My mom called waking me up with news of a bombing. What in the everlasting FUCK?!?!

I rolled over and grabbed the remote off the wooden headboard of my king-size waterbed, causing my three boxers sleeping around me to all look up at me disturbed. The TV showed me what my mom was describing, in vivid and graphic technicolor.

I want to interrupt here and remind you that this was a time in America before high school shootings were heard of and before known terrorism groups and planes flew into towers. Had horrible, scary things occurred? Of course, I remember the news scrolling with the Unibomber, serial rapists and murderers like Richard Rameriz and Ted Bundy. I watched in horror as Jeffery Dahmer was taken away and then the famous ice chest full of body parts was removed from his apartment building as revolted neighbors stood by. The difference was these were terrible instances against people, but none had been of the magnitude and hatred at this scale.

This was before words like "defund the police," "MAGA" (make America great again), and "woke" were common in daily conversation. The Cold War was not a very distant memory, there had been the Gulf War and a lot of instability around the world. (Side note, I think sometimes when people talk about the past, they say things about how good things were and how they want to go back, but this is not one of those discussions. Sometimes we forget that every generation or decade has their beautiful moments and bad moments, and if we sensationalize another time, it takes away from the moments that pass by.) So, in 1995, when we heard words like bombing and terrorism, it was not even a consideration that those were things that could occur on American soil. That kind of thing happened in places with funny names far from home—USSR, Somalia, North Korea—not smack dab in the very center of America, just a few miles from the exact center (geographically) of the United States of America!! Maybe we thought there was a forcefield around us. Maybe we were so narcissistic that we thought no one would dare. Or maybe we did not think the first time it would occur would be from within our borders. Meanwhile, however, the cracks in the foundation of AMERICA were occurring, kinda like when an addict starts using drugs, or when an alcoholic starts drinking. The cracks were growing and this was the first time we all saw and felt it to our core.

The Oklahoma City Bombing changed all American lives because it woke us up to the very real threats posed by domestic terrorism.

And it also unashamedly and transparently showed its ugliness to everyone who tuned in for the evening news.

Did you know Oklahoma City was not even on the weather station map before the Bombing? Again, this was 1995 and MapQuest (which now is antiquated) wasn't even available. If you drove, there were paper maps. If you were lucky, you had a large Thomas Guide map book, and if not you were unfolding and folding large maps to try and see in front of you as you read the map!

There was no app to check the weather; it was either the evening news, your grandpa's knee, or the Weather Channel.

THE CALL

"Are you getting called up?" My older sister Tina asked me over the phone before I could say hello. "I heard on the news that they were calling up the National Guard and I knew you just joined so I was worried."

I leaned against the kitchen wall, holding the receiver attached to the long telephone cord, wishing it stretched all the way to the living room where I could sit. (Remember I mentioned those moments when you just know this will be a turning point in your life? Well, this was one for me.)

"No, they haven't called and I do not think they will," I responded, trying to sound confident, and thinking it was weird that she would have seen anything about the Oklahoma National Guard in California. "I mean, I'm all the way in Lawton and that's like a hundred miles away from OKC."

"Well, take care and let me know. I love you."

"I will. Love you too."

I hung up the phone, not realizing the call would actually take place. Now, let me chime in and say, I do not recall how many hours or days it was before my commander telephoned and said I was being called up to

23

help identify the victims of the bombing. I do not want to get ahead of myself here, but for literally over TWO decades I remembered this time in my life as weeks, when actually it was only three days onsite. It is crazy how a brief period of time can create so much change and how our memory can think one thing but reality is totally different. Talk about crazy, huh?

"SPC Mangini, I need to let you know that if you feel you are not able to do this assignment, I will call the next soldier and—"

"No, sir, you can count on me. I will be there."

So, here's the thing. I joined the Army to see the world, became a combat medic. Born-to-kill, trained-to-save. Hoorah! I certainly was not going to let any opportunities to do what I had been trained for pass me by!

I did not listen well to what my commander said though. I thought, help out with some victims as in individuals who have been hurt not killed.

You, my awesome reader, are probably already realizing that people who are just hurt could tell you who they were and what was hurting. I was so young and not ready for this obtrusive change to my life. I thought (like anyone else who is 20ish and healthy) that I was ready to tackle anything and everything.

I thought I had already figured out how this whole life thing would go. This was something I think no one was able to prepare for, especially me.

Yeah. About that...

The Armory and a Friend

April in Oklahoma is a tricky time of the year. The Robin birds are starting to venture out, being the first birds to show each year. The morning sun shines but does not have the warmth of spring yet and most days begin with an icy dew. Afternoons can get really warm and this is usually the beginning of windy spring which spells tornado season. Think about it like this: heater in the car on the way to work and AC when you leave work for lunch or maybe just your ride home, and always the possibility of a tornado right before bed.

Our unit commander was waiting to meet with us at 0700 that morning. I had only been there one time, just a month before to sign paperwork and swear in for my service contract. I did not have a map or any G.P.S. navigation (of course). I remember taking a wrong turn, getting lost, and being so flustered that when I stopped at a highway McDonald's for coffee, I paid with a twenty-dollar bill instead of the five dollar bill I meant to grab and left without getting change! I did not realize until I went to lunch later that day, and by then, it was too late to try to figure out which McDonald's I had stopped at. I remember that day like it was yesterday, only now I realize maybe the clerk needed the extra fifteen dollars more than me.

The old, red brick armory sat at the end of a half-mile paved, blacktop driveway, off the intersection of NE 23rd & Air Depot in Midwest City, Oklahoma.

Stark, bare trees and bitter cold surrounded me. The chill of the air sank through to my bloodstream. (Again, with the cold! Ugh!)

It was barely days after the bombing and we were being briefed on how this deployment would work. There would be two crews in total; the first crew had started on April 20th and was already feeling overwhelmed and ready to switch out. We would work 12-hour shifts, be stationed at the Medical Examiner's Building located three blocks from the now obscenely cratered federal building.

My plan of leaving active duty (in January) was to move to the OKC area in May or June that year, so like I said, I still lived in Lawton. I had only been to our armory once to complete the in-processing into the Oklahoma Army National Guard the month before, and I did not know anyone yet, other than the commander and unit clerk who had done my paperwork. Also, since I was the only one who did not live locally, the commander offered to let me sleep in the armory in between my shifts. Just as the thought of sleeping alone on an Army cot wrapped in an itchy wool blanket started to create a lot of anxiety inside me, a woman interrupted the commander, "She will not sleep here alone, that's just creepy!"

(Oh, my sweet baby Jesus!!! Bless you, my inner voice shouted.) She turned to me and continued with her beautiful (heavenly music to my ears) loud voice, "You are coming to stay at our house! My family and I have plenty of room."

I wanted to hug her, but refrained, still maintaining my professional soldier persona. (I mean, I had to look cool, calm, and collected.) She and her family lived fifteen minutes away, so we just drove together. It was nice getting to know someone who soon became an awesome friend. I just did not know it yet.

TRIGGERS

I keep saying, "Remember, this was a different time," and maybe it is a little annoying. I feel like sometimes when we look back at a time in our life, we forget all the minute details that are different.

For example, in 1995, the cell phone was a phone without a cord attached to a wall. There was no camera, no one texting... That being said, I am mentioning this to show how different our lives are today. I am literally authoring this book on my cell phone! If someone wants to show anything to anyone, it can happen almost immediately. Take a video of something terrifying or fascinating (or any cute kitten, dog, or sloth) and watch it go viral. If someone had shown me what social media is today, I wouldn't have believed them.

***

This is going to be a little graphic, so skip this section if you need to.

So, back to the Medical Examiner's Office in April 1995...

The front of the building faced the street and had the boring look of a state government building. The drab waiting room and small reception area gave way to double doors that opened into hallways, which led to the back of the building where sterile-looking suites were used for determining cause of death. I gathered it would have been a very non exciting place to work most days and nights. I remember the night security guard there was one of the first women I ever met who always had a huge dip of chewing tobacco in her lip, and not Skoal either. I'm talking about that big pouch of tobacco! She was probably just working there to skate through the last years before retirement, and I hoped retirement came soon after all of this mess.

There was a large, open space coming from the clinician's suites and a walk-in freezer with a huge, looming door. Off to the side were a few more small rooms with windows in the doors, and you had to stand on your toes to see through. Between those rooms, there were a couple of long tables, then there were the bay doors. Outside was the dock and a slanted walkway leading to three parked semi-trailers, two of which housed victims who were recently recovered.

One of my duties was to assist in the identification process of the victims; another duty was to bring whatever numbered black bag from the back of the cooled truck the examiner requested into said examination room. This sounds easier than it was.

All the bodies pulled from the wreckage were placed in black body bags, and white paint had been used to number each one. Each one was numbered in the order they had been collected from the bombing site. (Picture large black bags, ranging in thickness, each with a large painted white number.) They were laid in two or three rows across and lined the entirety of both trucks, spaced so that there was room to maneuver around. One thing I never knew before this experience was that body bags only come in one size.

However, one size does not fit all. Some of the bags were "full" or had a thick lump, like there was an adult zipped inside, while others were flattened with a smallish-sized lump at one end. We all knew there was a child inside.

Because it was April in Oklahoma, the trucks had built-in air-conditioning units and were dreadfully cold and loud. It was so cold inside that the bags would stick, and any bodily fluids would make it harder to pull up from the metal grooves which made up the floor inside the trailer.

The National Enquirer was rumored to offer $10,000 for any pictures taken at the medical examiner's office. There was a parking garage located less than a block from the Examiner's Office. Someone standing on the top floors could use a high-powered camera and would have been able to get some decent pictures if they so desired. This made my job even more difficult because I was the one climbing into the trailer and then using a flashlight to see the white numbers. When I found the number that I was looking for, I would pick up the body bag, place it on a gurney, and wheel it into the exam room to then assist with any method of determining the identity that was needed.

Okay, wait. I just walked through that like it was normal. Let me tell you, nothing was normal, and none of it was easy.

Intently looking for numbers on body bags inside a fairly dark trailer is not fun. Add the photographers trying to snap that $10k shot and one of the truck doors having to stay closed at all times, too. We worked in pairs, but Oklahoma is known for wind, so one person would stand inside at the edge, holding one door shut and trying to let as much light in with the other door while trying not to let both of them be shut, thus plunging both living and deceased into darkness... really dark darkness. One problem—well, way more than one—was when I or whoever was inside with the flashlight would find the appropriate body bag, they were not easy to pick up and carry. Quite the opposite. So, there goes someone holding the door. And let's not trip on the way out. Yes, the whole thing sucked a lot.

I am not saying this to be disrespectful or crass, and actually, if you have spent any time with a seasoned nurse or combat medic, you'll agree our humor is so very dark. When we'd be waiting for the next doctor or test results, we would joke about things that anyone else would have been aghast to hear. Again, I don't mean to be rude, but when you have to pick up a small child or toddler who is wrapped inside an adult-sized body bag, the humor has to match the severity.

So, we nicknamed ourselves the BBDC—Black Bag Drag Crew.

Side note: Obviously a sick attempt at humor and is not meant to disrespect the humans or the situation.

Back to the National Enquirer wanting to get that money shot so it could be what everyone standing in line at Safeway would see perched next to the Snickers bars. Everyone thought I was teasing when I said I would take a picture of my ass in the ladies' room and sell it!

(Good thing we did not have smartphones yet.) By the way, they never got a good shot, and I think a fence was quickly installed, causing them to stop harassing us.

People smell differently when they die peacefully versus from trauma. When someone has lived a long life and passes while surrounded by their loved ones, peacefully and blanketed in love, the person just dies, there is no identifiable smell of death. When it is an accident or murder, any horrific situation that ends a person's life and their time on this earth, it is totally the opposite. I am unsure of the exact science or physiology. Still, there is something about the sudden release of hormones and fear, the mix of anxiety, pain, or horror, perhaps with the knowledge that they are about to die, no reset button or extra lives left, nope, the person is dead and no longer alive.

I will not go further into detail, and I am not sure if there is a correct grouping of words that would describe or be able to convey exactly what the smell consists of. Still, I can tell you, it is a smell that can invade my nasal passages and call to attention every cell in my body, stop me in my tracks, and even devastate me, slamming me back in time to that cold coroner's office in Oklahoma City back in 1995.

Like I stated at the top of this section, I now know this is called a trigger.

***

I am not authoring this book to have a political discussion or talk about Timothy McVeigh, Terry Nichols, or the Branch Davidian Compound. This is about what I lived through and witnessed, smelled, felt, tasted, and touched and how I can still step into those trailers in my mind today. Talking about triggers, I have worked on "getting over," "dealing with," and "letting go," but some things still won't go away. The one that still gets me triggered is Vicks VapoRub. I have had the physical reaction of almost vomiting just from seeing a little jar of Vicks. Each time I heard a commercial for Vicks VapoRub, I became so angry or feel physically ill. For over twenty years, I did not understand why. I felt so foolish because everyone would talk about how comforting and wonderful that stupid little jar was to them, and I wanted to throat-punch anyone who had one around me. So why such a volatile response? Because of the unpleasant smells, many of us rubbed Vicks on our upper lips. We also rubbed it inside the N95 masks we wore just to ensure they worked. It did until it did not, and then it was the horrible combination of the smell of death mixed with Vicks.

I know my mom rubbed Vicks on my back when I was young, but I honestly do not remember when I could smell it or even see the jar and not have a physiological reaction.

***

There were 168 body bags. Remember the tables I mentioned? There were red biohazard bags of different sizes, all with various body parts not attached to the person who woke up with them the morning of April 19, 1995.

DNA samples from all victims and all the various body parts were collected and then (hopefully) painstakingly matched.

One of the most incredible duties we were part of would be to match a limb to the correct body or place it into the proper body bag, allowing the individual to be respectfully put to rest. We had a large paper poster or whiteboard that had numbers and names corresponding to each other, and it would be bittersweet when we could cross a name completely off, meaning we had correctly identified and also confirmed that all found parts were in one place. It has always bothered me that there was a leg that did not match (even through DNA) any of our victims.

***

Cartoons

Yes, a stupid cartoon was my saving grace when I would get to Gretchen's house, drinking my tall boy Coors Light or Bud Light after my hot burning shower trying to take the smell of death off me, out of my pores and my sinuses.

Her family was extremely kind and accommodating but their family dog was not so much. He was an Akita and loved his family. He was not accommodating, not friendly, and certainly not happy that I was there.

Maybe it wasn't me he did not like. I mean, dogs always like me. Maybe it was that smell I was trying to scrub off. I do not know. All I know is I was grateful the bathroom was attached to the guest room!

THAT DAY

At 9:02 am on April 19, 1995, a bomb exploded.

It started as a normal Wednesday morning when the small Midwestern city suddenly collapsed and shattered into chaos and despair.

Oklahoma was a flyover state (yes, it was huge in oil production and was the birthplace of a lot of ideas and people), but the weather channel did not even have it listed on national television. Until this. How sad is that?

I cannot see a clock without seeing 9:01 and 9:02. It is the difference between a bomb and normalcy. The difference between life and death. I still cannot NOT be triggered when I look at a clock and see 9:01 and 9:02; it still stops me.

You might be thinking why would the time 9:01 bother me, I mean, 9:02 sure- that is when the bomb went off, makes sense. The minute before though, that one actually twinges the nerve endings in my gut a bit deeper. It signifies the difference of a simple life. However, as I write this, I know that it was a perception of a simpler time, even though really, it was not that much different. It is the difference between a bomb and normalcy. The difference between life and death.

When I use the stairs, I picture masses of people struggling to run out of a blackened burning pile that was a building moments before. When I use the elevator, I picture it slamming to a stop and pitching into blackness. But how do you live? Pretty much every building everywhere except single-story homes have a stairwell or elevators. The worst ones are the ones at the VA medical facility I work at, because it is so average, so normal, regular, boring, vanilla - beige. So much like those boring government-looking buildings, especially the Murrah building. I would guess that no one went there because they wanted to see the sites. No, they went because they had adult stuff to do. Legal things, hard or expensive stuff that wasn't all that fun. I'm sure the men and women who held jobs there had their work friends, work hubbies, or bffs who knew that on Wednesday, so and so would always bring donuts from Brown's Bakery up the street.

I picture those masses of people struggling to run out of a blackened burning pile that was a building moments before.

That wonderful, boring lull of complacency being able to drop the kids off at the daycare downstairs, go flirt at the coffee machine (no Starbucks or Dutch Bros in Oklahoma at that time), then tell tall tales of whatever sporting event was going to be playing that night on CBS or NBC, before finding the assigned cubicle to actually do a bit of work before noon.

How horrifying it must have been to try to find the exit, not knowing what had happened. Was it totally dark? Or was there only bright sunlight shining through where a solid wall had just been?

I wonder if people were being loud or deathly quiet. What about the people who had mobility issues or were injured but cognizant enough to know to get out?

Yeah, that's what I think of when trying to run down to get a snack between meetings. I imagine that day vividly, still haunted by the images of the rubble and destruction that followed the horrific explosion. I mean, how can I not?

Back to Reality

I returned to my normal life, unaware that things inside me had changed. My birthday was the next month, in May. The coolest thing on the shelf that year was a pair of Bose speakers, and guess what I opened? Man, I was so excited! They got hooked up immediately, and the house was pumping. liquor and beer were flowing, and people were dancing around, being young and having fun. Pretty sure there were keg stands and general good ol' American fun being had by all. In fact, everything was awesome until my buddy tripped and knocked one of the speakers, scratching the side of it.

Now, it did not damage the actual speaker, it was only a cosmetic scratch, but you would have thought by my reaction that the world had just ended. I did not recognize myself as I ranted on and on about how inconsiderate and stupid they were. I was not the type to berate someone like this, especially a friend and for something so trivial. I did not recognize myself and I really did not like the person I was seeing.

What I did not know was that something inside me was different.

***

In 1995, we didn't know about PTSD. Some doctors were starting to talk about it, but it wasn't common knowledge to the general public. It certainly was not to a now-decorated US Army soldier who could do more pushups than anyone she knew, and was pretty cocky about... well, everything.

No Coincidences

My cute, shiny black boot had a scuff. Ugh. As a former Army soldier, this was a pet peeve of mine, especially when I was receiving a prestigious award from the state at the iconic National Cowboy & Western Heritage Museum, which back then was the Cowboy Hall of Fame.

A little about this awesome place, from what I have learned over the years... The museum was created in the late fifties to celebrate the lives of people, or cowboys, from the Midwest who had lived extraordinary lives. Most of them were men, but some women, names like Gene Autry who was the golden boy of Oklahoma and rightfully so. Also, Chester A. Reynolds who was originally from Kansas City but founded the Hall of Fame and whose name is on an award given out each year to people who contribute to the preservation of American West history. Another award is the bronze statue (and I believe it is a really cool one!). Recipients have included John Wayne, Tom Selleck, Roy Rogers, and Gene Autry.

That being said, I was surprised to not only be invited to the awards event but I would be invited as an awardee! As I stood in the grand hall, surrounded by statues and photographs of legends, I couldn't shake the unease over my blemished boot. Of course, it was not like anyone could see the scuff, it was on the inside of the black leather, just above the rubber sole. My brain's voice wondered when it could have happened. Probably when I was walking from the car, it was an exceptionally long walk to where I had parked, the back lot to the already large parking lot. That went into another tirade in my head; if we were receiving awards, shouldn't there be special parking privileges? I wondered how many people were receiving these once-in-a-lifetime awards. I didn't feel like I belonged there with all these heroes.

I was simply doing my job, humbled and proud to be called upon for my country. Still, the honor felt surreal, sharing the stage with such illustrious company. There were so many people there who deserved such recognition. And the place was beautiful, almost magical, in a cowboy kinda way!

It was a dinner event, and I made my way to the tables, elaborately decorated and neatly arranged. I noticed a few people had taken their seats, many others were just mingling, shaking hands, and hugging, with drinks in hand. A noisy buzz of conversation filled the room as the excitement steadily built. Finally, an announcement came to find our seats, and when I sat down, I met my table mates. The man next to me looked slightly familiar, like I knew his face but had never had conversations with him. His name was Trooper Charles Hanger and he was the Oklahoma Highway Patrol officer who arrested Timothy McVeigh. It struck me as funny, not ha-ha funny, but you know, funny that he had not seen himself as a hero. If he had not been paying attention and doing his job well, he might not have pulled McVeigh over or noticed the missing tag on the vehicle's license plate. Subsequently, McVeigh could not show proof of ownership, was found with a handgun on his person, and was arrested. He had not been tied to the worst terrorist attack on American soil, but he would be while still in custody at 201 N. Shartel Avenue in Oklahoma City.

Of course, I know the address of the Oklahoma County Detention Center well since it was my residence for a while (years later of course), and another thing, when they finally knew who they had in custody, they did not want to risk assassination as it was too much of a safety risk, so they constructed a new courtroom in the basement of the jailhouse. The normal courtrooms were at the courthouse about six blocks away, where prisoners were transported by van. Years later, this was the courtroom I was in when the woman from the D.A. told me I was looking at prison time. I broke the rules of never crying in jail, yes, I straight up broke down, tears streaming down my face and blubbering like a child. I remember saying something about how I was a veteran and this was not how I thought I would end up.

She stopped me and asked, "Wait, are you telling me that you are a veteran?"

"Yes, and I helped with the clean-up of the bombing," I sobbed out, the flood of emotions continuing, I did not care if my fellow inmates could see me blubbering.

Her eyes bore into mine and suddenly we connected. She said, "My brother was a veteran and I helped him get help from the VA. He thought he didn't need any help but he was suffering as an addict." And with what we now know as PTSD.

She had stepped in and told him that if it had been the Army that fucked him up, she was going to make sure the VA was there to help fix him. Somehow, I stopped crying, realizing that this woman was seeing and hearing me, that someone was on my side. Was I getting help?

Was I not going to go to prison? Yes, this person was instrumental in getting me involved with the Veterans Diversion Court. I realized that it is the small steps that make the most difference sometimes in our lives, and this was one. It was only one step, however, and I had many more to go before I made the right decisions.

KINDNESS

K nock knock. I looked to my left side, eyes blurred from sleep, widening quickly when I saw the policeman.

"You can't sleep here," he said after I rolled the window down.

I had pulled my truck into a stall at a nondescript car wash off NW 23rd street in OKC. I knew the area well, often having to pull in to quickly hit the pipe, but this time, though, I just wanted somewhere well-lit to chill and it was well lit.

As the reality of the situation seeped in like the freezing air through the window, my anxiety and panic escalated. I was not worried about a search; I did not have any drugs on me. Like I said, I was asleep. I had a warrant for FTA, failure to appear, an ongoing issue for me during this period of my life. I had a bad habit of not showing up for my appointments with the courts, which would then have a judge who would have to be alert the judge that I was not doing what I said I would do. Subsequently a warrant would be issued. It was not a good cycle of life.

"Yeah, you have to find somewhere to go, but go somewhere safe, okay?" His kind eyes connected with my dark brown eyes, probably wide with fear. I feared jail but really, anytime I went, I was okay. I mean, I was unhappy about losing my freedom, but I could catch up on much needed sleep.

He turned and walked away, breaking my speeding thoughts. I looked across the bench seat, assorted items like my black jacket and blanket pushed aside, my hoodie that was rolled into the perfect pillow and must have fallen to the floorboard when I woke up.

The elation hit me as I started my truck, a smile creeping up as the ignition roared to life. He had to have guessed by my reaction that I had a warrant but maybe he did not want to do paperwork or he just figured I needed a break.

I would like to say that I took the opportunity to do the smart thing and take care of the warrant, but you already know that was not the case.

BROKEN

One of the reasons I am authoring this book is that I want to help others by shedding light on experiences I have had, because they are examples of how female veterans can be overlooked and how services or resources that are available and have tremendously helped so many sometimes do not deliver. I am not sure if it is a system error or a human error, but I am going to talk about when the housing lady from the VA told me I couldn't be helped with any housing. Yes, they understood I was homeless and yes, they absolutely felt bad for me, however, because I was female and my dear friends Mark and Steven had let me stay at their house, I wasn't eligible for help. Mind you, my friends only housed me for two nights.

I was standing in the only place I had found that was warm, the Biltmore Hotel's laundry room. Because someone had left the door open, I snuck in and closed the door, grateful for the leftover heat from the dryers. My heart shattered. I had spent the last two nights in a beautiful, wonderful clean and safe spare bedroom at their home, waking in a room like an Ethan Allen showcase. I was pretty sure the thread count was high and I was not! I had showered and scrubbed clean, and washed my hair with shampoo and conditioner! I had eaten well, washed my few items of clothing, and had a glimpse of a 'normal' home with plenty of food, electricity, and love.

Let me back up just a tad. I had finally called the homeless hotline for the OKC VA. The location of the VA hospital was almost exactly across the street from the coroner's office where I had helped identify the men, women, and children who were victims of the bombing. I already mentioned I would avoid that area of downtown and this included the VA.

But I was so tired, exhausted, and cold... so bitterly cold. I finally had given up my stubbornness and asked for some help, which opened the door to questions I knew were going to be asked about my addiction, my drug of choice, and the whole can of worms so to speak. I was ready, and now, I had been shot down. Walls went back up and my Taurean stubbornness went to high gear. Fuck this.

With the rain dripping through the tent, the scene looked like something out of Lost Boys, that cool lair the vampires lived in. But it smelled odd, of rotting vegetation with sweet undertones mixed together, probably because of the salvage yard sitting just above with large slabs of concrete haphazardly stacked against the ground and covering the small incline above my makeshift home. I had denounced society. My phone had been stolen or thrown and broken, I don't remember. Either way, I had no phone, but I was fine with that. I had found this spot that others had abandoned, alongside carelessly thrown trash. I collected the rubbish and threw it all in a nearby dumpster. I may have been angry with the world, but I didn't want to live in filth. I had moved to one of the cleaner tents and set up camp with a cot and blankets. There were about five or six of those 5-gallon water bottles within all the ripped tents. Scattered old belongings, probably stolen and shifted through while someone was blasted off, looking for trinkets and shiny objects. I found a commercial building about a mile away from my new squatting space and once a week I would push a cart down a pothole-riddled, sad-feeling road to the building and fill up my bottles, never surprised but always annoyed when water would splash out on the way back because the thin worn tires were no match for the seemingly endless craters in the pavement. I would fill them up and look around for anything I could make money on at the salvage yard–cans, bottles, or whatever was available. I was not a good candidate for being homeless. For one, I am terrible at being dirty. I cannot stand to have my hands dirty, to have my fingernails unkempt, or see dirt or grime underneath, which was inevitable being I was now basically camping as my existence.

The cart would not allow itself to be pulled or pushed into the thick dirt between the road and my campsite, no matter how much I swore at it. So, in the last 400 yards, I lugged the damn things. Water always ending up sloshing out and soaking my dirty, ripped blue jeans or whatever T-shirt I had on. By the time I was done, all the bottles were placed in a neat row against the perimeter behind the tent. There was a blanket I laid across them to keep bugs and debris out of the openings. Most of the water was still inside the bottles and I was fairly happy with the fact that it would be at least a few days before I made the trek again.

Drip, drip, drip. What the crap?! I woke up to the sound of water dripping from the ceiling of the tent. I always thought these were waterproof! I remembered there was a tarp I had been cleaning up to use as a floor to my 'kitchen' area, so I got up, pulled my still-laced new-to-me New Balance sneakers on my bare feet (I cannot sleep with socks on!) and unzipped the tent door. Icy rain soaked me immediately as I scurried around in the night, gathering my tarp and some cordage. Through shivers and squinted eyes, I assessed the situation, realizing the tarp wouldn't be big enough to cover the tent completely, but it was all I had.

Have you ever attempted to throw a soaking wet outdoor tarp over the top of a tent, while large raindrops smacked you on your head? It felt like a monsoon, wind blowing and muddiness surrounding me and my little tent. Somehow, by the grace of God, the tarp was in place and secured. I felt like the llama crying in "The Emperor's New Groove" as I made my way into the tent and stripped out of my soggy clothes. After somewhat drying off and putting on a cleaner set of clothes (and socks this time) I laid on the cot, underneath the pile of acquired blankets, gripping the pearl handle of my 9-inch Bowie? knife that was under the pillow, and tried to get warm. The situation sucked but at least the tarp kept the tent pretty dry.

None of my friends knew where I was. There was no one I interacted with. However, my small stash of dope was running very low and (hello) I was not going to be sober now! The rain had stopped a few days earlier, and I was glad because the camp area had dried out. My clothes were dry and since I had used one of the concrete blocks as a drying rack, they smelled like clothes off a clothesline. Just kidding, they were pretty stank, but they were dry anyway. Maybe there were a few good things I remembered from being in the Army. I started walking towards the dealer's place after placing my collection of items in the bin at the salvage yard and receiving my hard-earned cash, because, like I said, I was not going to do this outdoor and alone time sober.

Yet Another Situation I Found-Well, No-Put Myself In

I turned the corner too quickly and the duffel bag full of metal shifted on my back, causing me to lose my balance. I bit my tongue before the vocal cry left my mouth and tasted blood. Better to taste blood than to get caught being somewhere I was not supposed to be.

I heard footsteps and icy sweat covered my body, under my layers of grime-covered clothes.

My mind's narrator remarked that whoever it is could probably smell me since I was not quite sure the last time I had showered.

"Shut up!!!" I may have thought the words, but they might have slipped out loud. Shit. Could this night just hurry up and get any worse? I took a deep breath, eased back into the shadow of the stairwell, and pulled out my mace. The footsteps grew louder, echoing my heartbeat in my ears.

I had just acquired this mace. Usually I carried a barrage of knives on me, but they would get dropped or lost or more likely, stolen, so it was new to me. I had been 'gassed' more times in basic training than any human should be, but I had not ever been in control of engaging the red button.

I mean, it is not a hard concept; besides, I was a hardened soldier and now homeless, living on the streets, a new battlefield so to speak.

I twisted the small metal can around in my hand to find the red button, trying to be careful not to engage until the unknown boots carrying an unknown person came around the corner of the dirty stairway landing. I felt its weight in my hand, though, as the footsteps slowed, pausing just a few steps away. Finally, a figure appeared and I dodged out, engaging the spray and...

Two things happened simultaneously. I recognized the person in front of me and I sprayed the shit out of both of us with the pink can of mace. The pepper spray coated both of us, seizing our sinuses as we choked and coughed uncontrollably. My eyes wanted to come out of my body, sprout legs, and run away, but instead, gave me the sensation of bursting into small flames.

I did not do this whole street life thing well; in fact, it was mostly horrible and always more challenging than it needed to be. My buddy gasped and doubled over, clutching at her eyes. I groaned, and sputtering cuss words between coughs. I tried to help her up, blinking furiously against the invisible stinging nettles residing now across my face.

"Next time, warn me before you jump out like that!" She rasped, rubbing her eyes furiously.

"Next time, don't show up without telling me you are coming!" I retorted vehemently.

Our laughter broke through the agony, echoing off the grimy walls, a brief escape from the gritty reality we lived. Neither of us were supposed to be at the location, and, well, she was not good at this stuff either.

***

Back to the story and the late 1990s...

I relocated to the OKC metro area, worked at the Red Cross for about five years, and was honorably discharged from the National Guard, having fulfilled my initial military obligation. I bought a house after surviving an apartment fire while in my first semester of nursing school. Let me say, nursing school is stressful enough but throw running from a burning apartment building at 2 am the night before your first clinical– that will unhinge anyone.

The instructor was speaking to the class the day before our first clinical. I was excited, maybe a bit nervous and jittery, but ready to take vital signs and work with real patients. I was ready to pour through the large blue charts at the nursing home, dissecting the doctors' orders, nursing notes, and lab results. I learned how to create care plans and it was interesting to see how everyone could work together just to help someone. In some ways, I saw similarities in the teamwork I had learned to appreciate in the Army.

It felt a little silly to be a tad nervous. I had done patient care and worked extensively as a combat medic, but this was different. Now I would be the nurse!

I hope you never run from a burning building or deal with arson, come to think of it. Most of what I discuss are things I would hope no one goes through. Of course, we all have things we learn or live through and think, "Wow, I do not want to go through that again!"

I am going off topic, so returning to the nursing school first clinical... The instructor was happy to hear that I was okay and told me I was excused!

By the way, the instructors at Oklahoma State University Nursing Program were amazing and actually helped me purchase new books, materials, and scrubs when mine were destroyed!

***

My dad and my wonderful stepmom, Kris, helped me with the down payment on my first house. I lived there through the nursing program and the sold it to move into a brand-new house in a brand-new, adorable neighborhood. Picture Pleasantville, only not creepy, with a white picket fence and a Bradford Pear tree perfectly placed in the front lawn. I loved my house, I loved my job, and it was so exciting!

I graduated from OSU-OKC (Oklahoma State University-OKC campus) and got my first RN job at St. Anthony's Hospital in Oklahoma City. This was the same hospital the nurses and doctors ran out of to help when the bombing occurred. I thought it was funny that I would go to work there when I avoided the actual downtown area like the plague. I still did, because my house was north of the city, so I would drive in to work, park in the parking garage, work twelve hours inside the ICU, and go home. I avoided driving to that part of town, even if it was only a couple blocks away.

My family could not fathom why I hadn't just moved back to California. I did not have an answer. It wasn't that I did not want to go back or to come home. I always thought about it as an option, just never could act on it. The answer was always 'after I finish school' or 'after I have a little experience as an RN.' Finally, they stopped asking. Still, everything inside me felt like I was alone, always looking to find where I belonged. I felt empty even when I was becoming successful and appeared to be living my best life. I could not find the way.

Sleep, No Thank You

I hope you do not understand the meaning of "night terrors," although I'm sure most are familiar with the term. Also, there is also Google and any search engines that explain everything there is to ever know.

What I mean is that I hope you do not know the feeling of waking abruptly with panic, a cold sweat, and the feeling in your chest like the devil himself has his hands wrapped around your plural space, trying to constrict any expansion of your muscles as you try to breathe.

My first night terror woke me up like that. It occurred when the bomber attacked the Olympics in Atlanta, Georgia. I thought at the time it was just some crazy, random, scary dream brought on by the events I watched along with everyone else instead of some awesome physical sporting event. I actually did not know what it was and never guessed it would be the start of something that I have now battled for years.

***

I'm standing on the edge of a very tall cliff looking out into the ocean. It is dark. Nighttime. There is a full moon with a few perfectly-situated clouds overhead. It is the perfect temperature and the gentlest breeze barely touching my hair. It feels so wonderful. And THEN.

An enormous crash of some sort takes place. I do not know if something happens to me or if I am observing something horrible, all I know is loudness and chaos ensues. I am now half wading and half swimming in the salty waters, my world consumed by a strong undertow and a deep fear that I need to help–that I am the only one who is able to help whoever is in need. I keep trying to find them, whoever they are.

Something bumps my arm and I am now looking down (like a heavenly observer) at myself in the darkness of that seawater with just enough light to see what is happening and what keeps bumping into me are random body parts, none of which are my own. The little toddler leg. A giant man's hand with a championship football ring attached to the finger. A person's unremarkable torso. A woman's manicured hand, nails still polished but with dirt and grime around the edges.

I note that it is weird to see that in the water, and I wake up, more frightened than if I had woken up to a stranger in my room. I think the reason I would be less frightened in that situation is that I know how to defend myself. I would recognize that there was something wrong and I would be able to defend myself or any bed partner. This was a fear that was very unknown. Who was I supposed to help and what was I supposed to do?

One thing I knew was I recognized the manicured hand, and as I started to dissect my night terror, I recognized many of those parts from the time spent identifying the victims of the 1995 bombing. Each body part carried a story, a person with a life that had been violently ended by that tragic event.

I did not know they were a "norm" for people with PTSD, that anything was a "norm" for people like me. I just knew I did not like them and the feeling I would carry through the next day—like I had traveled to hell and somehow crash-landed back in my bed.

COFFEE SHOP VIBE

This chapter is a shoutout to a small coffee shop I frequented during the late 1990's in Oklahoma City called Diversion. Picture these words spoken like open mic night where the audience and the speaker are in sync and the vibe just flows. I would like to say that if the coffee shop was there today on 1745 NW 16th in Oklahoma City, these are the words I would say.

Homeless
   Addict
   JAIL
   Anger
   Years
   Cold
   Snow
   Ice
   Where to sleep
   Where to hide
   Liars

Thieves

Deal

Hood

Ghetto

The Flats

Tired

Streets

Copper pipes

Empty wallet, empty heart, empty stomach, empty houses, empty eyes, empty pipe, empty baggie, empty pockets

Alone

Scared

Angels

Hustle

Loss of RN

Lost my home

Lost my house

Lost my white picket fence

Lost my safety

Lost myself

Almost lost my life

No Sun = Low Vitamin Count, or Can I Get a Dorito, Please?

This section is about going to jail in May 2016 on an FTA (failure to appear). I was inside for six months, literally inside as in NOT going outside at all. Most jails are designed for the male population, like after the jail was built, the officials realized women can do things that are not ok in society and they, too, need a place to be locked up. Nice to be the afterthought.

There was nowhere dedicated to females getting to see the sun or walk around where we would be, I guess, unable to escape or be in view of male prisoners, so they just kept us all locked up. Once in a while we would go to the basketball court, which was still inside, frigidly cold, with no bathroom and no basketball. (What the crap!?) It always felt like a punishment to go to the basketball courts because time literally stopped when you walked in. I never knew how long I would just be sitting in there. It was the first place prisoners went when we got to our assigned pod, and let me tell you, in the movies when the new 'kid on the block' or 'tough ol broad' inmate walks into their new living situation for whatever assigned time, and they walk with arms stretched around neatly folded blanket, pillow, and other miscellaneous items—that, my friend, is not at all what I went through in reality. One First, there are zero pillows, unless you count the rolled laundry bag that's a quarter way full of your dingy long socks, bra, and underwear... and by the way, they are all previously worn by someone!

There were jobs that prisoners could have. We did not earn any money, but at least we had something to do. It was an opportunity to leave our cell and cell block. I got a job pulling canteen items and it was actually pretty fun; I got to see what people ordered because they had money on their books. Oh, the array of yumminess! I did not ever have any money on my books and on a daily basis would use some of my hustling skills to procure coffee. I did not have great hustling skills, however, and many times someone would just give me some out of kindness (or pity). Sometimes my assigned cellmate (Cellie) would have enough to spare. So, having a job in the canteen gave me the opportunity to see and sample (when no guards were looking) the aforementioned goodies, especially Doritos or The Whole Shabang Chips. (Amazingly yummy!)

It also allowed me to be part of the crew that got to take the trash out once which gave me the three or five minutes (maybe) of being physically outside the county jail building that summer of 2016.

Pulling canteen items meant I would take a piece of paper with the inmates' name, picture, and the items they purchased, place them in a tray and then stack the trays for distribution. So here is one thing, every one of us working had been caught committing some sort of illegal activity, so was anyone really surprised when they found out we snuck a bite of anything? One girl got the nickname "Milky Way" because the guard caught her with half the candy bar in her mouth!

I cannot describe what it's like NEVER BEING OUTSIDE, NOT SEEING THE SUN, AND NOT SMELLING FRESH AIR.

Too much? I want to convey how horrible and physically ill it makes someone to never go outside.

I woke up one morning after almost three months of being a resident of 201 North Shartel Ave aka smelly OKC Jail, with my brother Tony's phone number suddenly in my head.

If it were not for my wonderful brother Tony, I really do not think I would be here - especially here - to tell you about my journey. He was brave enough to tell me how fucked up I was and loving enough to always be there for me, even if it was just to let me hear his voice, while I sat in the Oklahoma County Jail that summer. I was so devoid of life. Once you've lived that life of addiction, there's no other feeling more powerful than that primal force to get high. You say you care, or love, or hurt, but everything is connected and controlled by "When am I going to get high?" Literally everything.

I would call Tony once a week and during those few minutes, I would listen to him talk about life with his family and our family, such normalcy that was so foreign yet, scar tissue seemed to be removed every time he spoke. I'd remember how much I loved him. And there was that time my mom treated the whole family, everyone was there, and my heart actually broke, but in a healing way. Maybe his voice and his words were the catalyst that I needed. I do not know.

What I do know and remember is that I wanted to continue moving forward. I started believing that I did not want to be in that fucked up zombie mode of not living life–for real this time, more than ever–and I meant it. Things began to change slowly, imperceptibly at first, like the slow unraveling of a thick, tangled rope. Of course, it helped that I was just sitting in jail for half of a year of my life! But during those long days confined within concrete walls, a clarity surfaced that I hadn't ever experienced in maybe ever. I realized that I was either going to die or learn to live.

WHAT DID I SAY?

She was pretty and wore a sleek outfit, very professional and very out of place in the jail. Her name was Jessica and I knew her from the Veterans Diversion Program. Jessica was there in front of me and suddenly, after sitting six months in Oklahoma County Jail, I was asking for rehab. I do not know if you are familiar with how all that stuff works. I certainly was not, and let me tell you, you do not just ask for rehab and they say okay, you can go tomorrow. Nope.

I asked and Jessica said something to the effect of, "Oh, shoot, there is not one for women in Oklahoma. We will have to figure something out. Maybe we can send you to Leavenworth."

So, I am pausing the story for a few tidbits of information, some of which I actually did not know until recently.

There are four cities in the United States named Leavenworth. I had only known of the Kansas location until I was exploring the Pacific Northwest and found Leavenworth, Washington. The other two states with a Leavenworth are Indiana and Minnesota. Kansas was the first, and will be the city in my story. (I do have new goals to visit the other Leavenworths in the future!)

Fort Leavenworth is the only U.S. Army maximum security prison, and it is located in Leavenworth, Kansas. I have a few more things I have learned about this prison, but this is not the time.

My heart stopped... literally stopped. Right there in that drab, cold ugly jail room, I wondered if this was for real? Was I going to the infamous Army prison? Was this going to be my existence, my life? I swear my arteries clamped shut at the thought. "Oh my Gosh, what?! No! I mean, is this for real? I am asking for rehab and you want to send me to the Leavenworth Prison?" My voice quivered and was at an extremely higher pitch than I meant it to. Her eyes quickly looked up from the papers in front of her and into my eyes.

Chuckling, she answered, "Oh, yeah, no. That is the just the closest rehab for females and veterans. I can see how that sounds." Still chortling, she picked the single sheets of paper together, combined them, and placed a medium black clip on the side before placing them in her attaché case.

My heart returned to a normal heartbeat. Also, I was perturbed but not enough to say something... well, maybe enough to say something stupid so as to cause this process to go slower than it already was if that was possible. She stood up and said she would be in touch when she had confirmation of my admittance to the Domiciliary in Leavenworth, Kansas. (Why did she have to keep saying Leavenworth? I still cringe at that word, so synonymous of being in trouble.)

Side note: While serving in the United States Army, if anyone did anything wrong, from jay walking to writing bad checks, they were said to be headed towards the infamous prison.

So, to someone who had spent a good amount of time in the Army, just the thought of the word created a great deal of anxiety!

Finally, after another long few weeks of waiting impatiently, word came that all I needed to do was find a ride to an inpatient rehabilitation center, or 'Domiciliary,' which I learned was a funny name for rehab, which is literally a state away from where I sat in the Oklahoma County Jail. I was incarcerated and unable to unlock the door, much less call an Uber and leave! Seriously? Yes. They were profoundly serious.

The woman sounded a bit frustrated on the other side of the call, she was saying something about the Diversion Program did not have the funds to send me to the rehab. They were really trying every resource but nothing was panning out. Did I have any resources I could use to find a way to get to Kansas? My heart was broken. I actually did not think this was possible since I had kept myself from actually feeling anything in my damaged and addiction-colored life. This sucked donkey butt.

I sighed to myself as I dialed my brother Tony's phone number. I already guessed his answer but I had to try, had to do something, anything to get out of this smelly, gross jail.

"What? No. No way, Jennifer," Tony said. "I am not giving you any money."

Well, that went exactly how I anticipated.

"But, Tony, I am not asking for money, just a bus ticket. The veteran diversion people told me I had to find my own ride." My Cellie and I exchanged glances–her up on the top bunk and wool blanket wrapped around her, back leaning against the concrete wall, and me standing awkwardly, ear against the phone receiver built into the wall phone (always about four inches lower than what would have been comfortable).

"That's bullshit, Jennifer! They wouldn't tell you to do that."

Ugh. I felt so dejected and scared. Also, looking back at the interaction, I would not have believed me either. I mean, come on, it sounded ridiculous. The waiting game continued. Days turned into weeks, my mundane existence was exactly that–mundane. Boring with a capital B. I read every book I could find. Have I mentioned that being in the county jail was nothing like what you see on TV? The phones, like I said above, have no cord. The receiver is built in. This is so no one gets angry and chokes someone else. This being jail meant there was no cool yard with cool-looking workout equipment and basketball courts with actual basketballs to play. It was an octagon-shaped pod, two floors, and each floor got out at contrasting times, which sucked because there were not a lot of people to hang out with. Of course, there had been too many fights when everyone was out of their cell but that was long before I ever was inside.

Finally, I was informed that someone in the Diversion Program had produced the funding (I actually think someone just bought the ticket feeling sorry for me), and that I would be leaving soon. Here's another thing that is frustrating... they never tell you exactly what day or time you are leaving. One day comes, looking much like the day before, and as you are sipping your long-awaited instant coffee, or maybe the clear coffee (hint: it's only plain water) when, "Mangini, let's go!"

Oh. Mylanta! Seriously? Yes, they were serious!

I gave my four-inch sleeping mat to someone, my wool blanket to someone else, grabbed the rest of my jail-issued clothing and small pile of correspondence and ran for the door. Freedom!

I was taken to the Greyhound station by sheriff deputies to be put on a bus to go to rehab. I had not eaten because I was out processing from jail so long that I missed breakfast and lunch. In between were threats of "you better show up at your rehab because there will be multiple warrants out if you do not show up!" from every guard I interacted with—the last while I was pulling my weathered black belt through the belt loops of my jeans that I hadn't seen in six months. (I told you, I cannot make this stuff up!)

The deputy who drove gave me $7 out of his pocket and the other deputy told me they provide meals and snacks on interstate drives (umm, they do not!). So here I am, dropped off hungry. I looked at the clock inside and realized I had about ten and a half hours to waste. I decide I can walk to my dealers and walk back in enough time. I start walking and about a block into my trek, a small pickup truck screeches to a halt and I hear "Jenn!" The voice belonged to Josh, the old running buddy who just happened to be driving by (coincidence, what?!) Ten minutes later, I knocked on my dealer's window and was greeted with hugs as I walked through the entrance of the doorway. Seconds later, I am getting high, and spinning pipe, laughing with the crew, sitting around like we always had, like no time had passed.

Sitting there in that living room, where I had spent so many hours over the last few years, was so unimaginably wonderful but so different at the same time. Wonderful because I was out of jail!! This was a safe and familiar place to me. More than once, I had made a hurried trek down the familiar darkened streets from the county jail, excited that I was (of course) out of that horrible place and really excited to sit on the comfy chair and get high. Like I said though, this was so different. I had not seen any of my friends (street family) since the Spring around Mother's Day (and my birthday) and now it was cold, almost snowing, almost Halloween.

I was in the company of people who were just like me, addicted and living with it, trying to live right, but always ending up in the same place saying how they were going to make that change and knowing they could not. The dealer bought me a pizza and told me she would give me a ride to the bus in a few hours. Josh had actually held onto my backpack from when we got locked up so I had a couple of personal things like my phone and some random stuff. It was so surreal and just... different.

Different because I was different. I stood to leave for the bus, took one deeper inhalation from that glass pipe, and set it down, careful not to burn my hand or the table, and knowing I was putting it down for the last time. There was a pebble piece of dope sitting there on the table and I could not resist. I grabbed it and swallowed it as I walked out the side door of that house.

My dealer gave me a ride back to the station, gave me a twenty-dollar bill, and said goodbye. I got on the bus and not surprisingly, was the only one who did not sleep all the way to Kansas City. I sat there knowing that this was the beginning of a real chance to be me and to find out who I really was. I realized it had been so long since I honestly did not know who the real me was, without a glass pipe and stolen lighter in my pocket. (Yeah, I always took the lighter!)

I want to say that I feel like it sounds so dramatic to write this and maybe I am being a tad overly dramatic but I want to convey something that I think a lot of people who are addicts experience. I knew I was making the change to become sober or 'clean' and yes, of course that is a step forward, but I was saying goodbye to the one constant I had allowed to be in my life for years, the only raw honest relationship I had allowed, even more than the relationship I had with myself. I knew it was time for a change, time to break free from the cycle I had been caught in for so long. It was a painful farewell, but it was also a crucial step towards reclaiming my life and finding a new path. I felt a mix of fear and determination as I walked away, but deep down, I knew it was the right decision. Also, I was really, really high. I mean, wasn't I about to be in rehab?

(Okay, so maybe the wrong thing to say, but I have learned to live totally and completely transparently and honest. But I am getting ahead of myself, so back to October 27, 2016.)

Acrylic paint on canvas I painted in 2020ish

Life Changes for the Better

"Y ou have a disease, but you are NOT the disease."

The older woman had the perfect combination of white-gray and dark hair. It, as well as her clothing, was worn in stunning fashion and she held herself in an air of grace and warmth. She was the first therapist who I opened up to, who listened, and whom I was able to convey the extent of the horrific tragedy that occurred in Oklahoma City, not to the state or the country, but within me.

It was a beautiful day, cold but beautiful. The white snow glistened outside the large bay windows of the Leavenworth, Kansas VA third floor conference room. If you have ever spent time in the Midwest, you will understand this. If you have not, you should go sometime, but I personally would suggest the fall, when there is no snow and less chance of tornados. Anyway, back to the story...

I was in a dual diagnosis rehab program. Every one of us in the room was a veteran and every one of us had an addiction and another diagnosis—PTSD, or Post Traumatic Stress Disorder.

I was sitting with men and women of all ages—crusty grey-haired old dudes from the Vietnam era, still arguing about ARMY vs. NAVY—some had walkers, some in wheelchairs, all with something to say.

We were addicts of all sorts—alcoholics, some homeless, all veterans—all completely fucked up.

There were men and women around my age and younger, oh so much younger! There were veterans who had been in the Gulf war, Afghanistan, OEF (Operation Enduring Freedom), and OIF (Operation Iraqi Freedom). Some seemed so young with bodies that should be full of youth but their eyes were as empty as mine. How on earth did I get there?

Life moved forward, like it does of course. I met some friends and worked on myself daily with the many therapists there to help us all. I found out that I was really talented at art through their Art Therapy Program. I was blessed to be part of a women's group where we all shared, laughed, and cried together... and ate a lot of chocolate! I even met someone who worked for the VA there who shared my last name! We never looked at how far out we might be related; it was not the appropriate time or place, but it was still really cool. One day, the social worker asked to see me and she asked if I had any identification, other than my veteran ID. The answer of course was NO, so she helped me submit a request for my birth certificate and then arranged for me to go to the local DMV office to get an ID card. It was not a driver's license, but I did not have a car so that did not matter. It was an exciting day for me because it was just one more step closer to becoming a viable member of society!

One of the veterans I met at the Leavenworth VA was Mr. Bush. His large voice would thunder down the Domiciliary halls along with his boisterous laugh. We became friends as we navigated the healing processes of therapy, and one day we had this interaction:

Mr. Bush said, "I want to buy you a phone."

"Umm, ahem, no thank you--and what the actual—" I stammered, taken aback by the unexpected offer. Why would he want to buy me a phone? Who was this guy?

I was in my first weeks at the Leavenworth Domiciliary and it was my new home, a place that was where I was learning to live again, really. The building was nice and I was pretty elated to have my own room—vastly different from 201 North Shartel Ave, OKC, OK aka County Jail! There, I had shared living space with at least two other incarcerated women, and living space being one room for everything, we could not control the lights, the temperature, or the doors.

Back there in Oklahoma county jail, I would say to the guards almost on a daily basis, "There's something wrong with my door!"

"What?"

"It's locked." Ha ha ha... commence eye rolls.

Okay, back to the story!

It was a typical military style living, only instead of going to work every day, we went to classes, and groups would line up for meds before breakfast and before going to bed. Anyway, I was done with people saying they would do anything for me because what they wanted in return was usually not in my favor, or anything I wanted to be part of.

Mr. Bush said it again, with sincerity in his deep voice, but I still recoiled. "Nope, no way, no thank you!"

I do not remember or maybe I will not ever know what made me stop and listen to him, but I did, and he was really speaking from his heart. He helped me by getting me a new cell phone and helped me get it turned on. He never wanted anything in return, other than simple platonic friendship. It still touches my heart so much that he just wanted to help. His act of kindness retaught or maybe reminded me that there doesn't have to be an ulterior motive for everything and everyone. His selflessness was a rare find in my broken-shattered world, and it even showed me that there were still good and genuine people in the world, giving me hope that even the smallest acts of kindness can have an enormous impact on someone's life.

Okay, now that being said, and I am not sure if I am feeling open or vulnerable or if I want to convey that I did have other people show me kindness, but this man's actions will always be a memory that makes me smile and also makes me want to do something for others. Pass it on, I guess.

***

It was in the early months of 2017, snow season was not over but it was in the last of the actual storm season. I was accepted into the Compensated Work Therapy (CWT) program working at the veteran's hospital! The CWT is a Department of Veterans Affairs (VA) clinical vocational rehabilitation program that provides evidence-based and evidence-informed vocational rehabilitation services. They partner with businesses, industries, and government agencies to provide veterans employment and labor support.

The position would not be as a nurse but I would be in the GI clinic and the area patients go before surgery. It was menial, stripping and making beds, making coffee for the doctors and nurses daily, filling the blanket warmer (everyone loves a warm blanket!), and–this was my favorite part–wheeling the veterans to their vehicles and thanking them for their service. I also was able to wear scrubs, just the boring hospital-issued ones but I was elated!

I knew it still wasn't enough, but the seed was growing. Would this be the closest thing to being a nurse again?

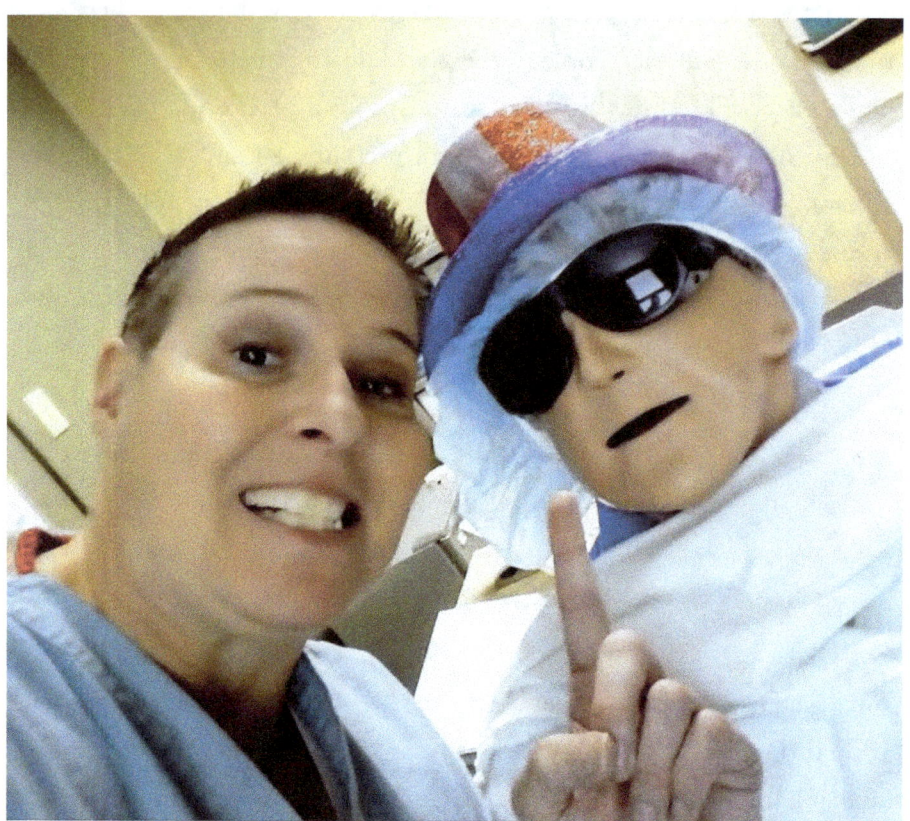

Having fun with the CPR dummy at Leavenworth VA hospital circa early 2017

Supportive

Support can refer to a variety of things, depending on the context. Here are a few common meanings:

* Physical support: This refers to holding up, sustaining, or bearing the weight of something. For example, a pillar supports a roof.

* Emotional support: This involves providing encouragement, comfort, or reassurance to someone. It can come from friends, family, or professionals.

* Financial support: This involves providing money or resources to help someone meet their needs.

* Moral support: This involves expressing approval, belief, or backing for a cause or person.

In essence, support means aiding or backing in various forms.

Sometimes support will be there when you don't want it but need it—like a bra. I mean technically I guess that can be a personal preference, but I would guess every woman I know (and don't know) has had the thought at least once about flinging her bra but had to leave it on because it's a societal thing.

**Ok enough of the bra talk, Jenn! **

I think where I am going with this is the support you'll receive from those closest to you will be steadfast and unwavering, often in your weakest moments when you might resist but ultimately need it.

Picture one of those name tags.

Hello
my name is

Stuck, Stubborn, & Not very nice.

Pretty much a description of anyone who is not interested in change but flying down the highway going the wrong way, so to speak. Support is like that stubborn name tag you wear, at times grating but offering clarity on the road of resistance.

Support is the presence that carries you through your darkest hours, lifting you when you're down and guiding you back when you're lost.

It's the unwavering presence that catches you when you stumble and anchors you when you're adrift.

For me, it is my relationship with my higher power, Jesus, and also, my connection with energy, knowing when I am in the right place.

It is also my lovely, amazing, beautiful wife, Laurie, who has been there when I have been in the worst way, and also on some of my best days. Someone once said that within the wedding vows, marriage is for better or worse, but not when it is harmful to one or both. I think there is a lot of wisdom there.

The other players in my support system are also so incredibly amazing and loving; it almost overwhelms me (in that wonderful, healthy way that makes crying so fulfilling and cleansing) because I truly was so far gone... and they were there with arms open when I came back! Did I mention my mom's ringtone for me is "Staying Alive"? I love our sense of humor. Now, such a terrible time has become a memory—never forgotten but accepting of all the intense work that has been accomplished.

All that being said, your support system cannot be the only thing that pulls you through; it is only a section of what you stand on—the biggest part needing to be standing on your own two feet. You must learn to balance on your own, discovering strength within yourself even as those around you lend their support.

***

Looking at this from a different perspective, have you ever tried to help someone stand up who is incapacitated or just doesn't want help? They might SAY they want to stand, but you know (when you are halfway between straining your lumbar muscles and finding out what a hernia feels like) that they are lying, or confused, or just think they have more physical ability than they actually do. They may have a physical problem standing or maybe they are just in the mood NOT to. Either way, you are only going to get hurt.

It is like that when you are a supportive player in this game, when the person needing help and support is playing, lying, or maybe just not in the place to receive. What a terrible place to be for both, but worse for the people watching, especially in the dope and PTSD, depression, and anxiety spiral. They are standing eyes wide open and memory banks filling up, full of disappointment and despair, while the main character nods off or blasts out into the cosmos, oblivious to the reality of pain. Of course when you do return, you have zero ability to cope and want to be zombies again.

It is a vicious and cruel cycle, AND—that's the thing with cycles—they spin endlessly until something, or someone, decides it's time to break free, or when the main player dies or ends up in prison, stuck on the yard until they are forgotten...

Still, the ones who truly suffer are those who stand on the sidelines, helpless and heartbroken.

That was a tough part to write, but again, life can be tough and painful. It also (and this is gonna be fun) can be beautiful and rewarding or exciting and empowering... so, so worthwhile. Going for a swim, having a new great niece say your name (OMGEE so cute!), waking up and drinking coffee... life is what you make it, and I am here to tell you that I am so grateful and blessed.

***

Have you ever had a bad Christmas? I mean, life happens right? Your dog jumps the fence or a close family member passes... maybe you spend the day in a hospital room or have the flu and stay home in bed. Regardless, the Christmas season affects everyone, even if the holiday you cherish is Hanukkah, Kwanzaa, or just celebrating family with Santa.

Not to go dark or anything, but my worst Christmas was spent sitting in an empty duplex that was more abandoned and squatted-in than empty. It was somewhere to crash out or get high. It was not pretty, not clean, and no place anyone wanted to be, just somewhere people ended up or stopped in, either to sell something, buy something, or be inside for a while.

Being on the corner of an intersection in the hood meant there was always traffic and always something going on. One night, someone named Princess had tagged the street in bright pink construction spray paint, with the word Princess taking up the entire width of one street. I remember that well because right after she did that, the neighbor's (a Mexican family who owned a highly successful construction company and also the huge place next door) small dog was hit and run right on the bright pink lettering. It was terrible. The kids and dad were outside when it happened right in front of them. The dad jumped in one of their cars and chased the guy down. I'm fairly sure he caught him, but I didn't witness it.

What I did witness was me dropping my just-opened tuna pack (which was my one meal for the day) and having the tuna mixed with water splash up on my calf as I ran out to the street after seeing the little brown fluffy dog go under the first tire. People are just cruel sometimes.

So back to the not-so-jolly Christmas Day, 2014 or 2015, but definitely not 2016! (I was in recovery for that one!!) First off, it was snowing and icy. I was so tired of being cold. So tired of trying to walk around in worn-out sneakers stolen off people's porches some random time ago. So tired of being hungry and broke, of carrying everything in my old blue backpack, including toilet paper to be used at places like this.

There was a small pile of white, crystal shards on the short coffee table. I was sitting in the large, oversized, threadbare chair—the only one in the room. At one time, it was probably extremely comfy, but now it was just okay... a place to sit that, if I angled my body right, some much needed sleep would occur. I had been keeping a blanket hidden in one of the closets, but like everyone and everything during this time of addiction, it never stayed long. There was no electricity or water on at the duplex, but the front room was well lit by the streetlight on the corner. It did not help with the cold though, excluding for the fact that there were solid walls and actual glass in the windows. The fact that there was no water was actually a good thing because roaches follow the water, and I do not like bugs or anything that can crawl their silky-smooth, creepy little legs across my arm in the middle of the night and wake me up. I had a shiver run through me, a memory of a stupid roach. It was gross to use the bathroom in a place like this, with no running water, but my trusty backpack always had a bottle stashed away.

There was a person on the couch and they were asleep; they had nodded off a few hours ago while dividing up their stash, and it put me in a really awkward situation. He snored lightly; stolen sneakers still flat on the dirty carpet of which the original color was never to be known. The morning sun shone through the dirty windows, thick enough glass that there was no ice inside the pane, and across the room from me, behind the couch, a non-working gas fireplace seemed to laugh at me in an odd, inanimate way.

The stash was not mine so I had not touched it. I really wanted to, but I did not want to deal with any consequences of my actions, so I sat and waited, guarding him and the alluring stash.

My Phone Rang

Has anyone ever loved you so much they gave you a house?

Let me tell you, it is a beautiful experience—very mind blowing to actually think I am so loved. I bet you are expecting a story now. Here we go!

My white "government" phone rang. I hesitated. Almost everyone who had the number were people I needed to stay away from if I were to stay in recovery, out of prison, and alive.

Still, I was excited to get a phone call since I had been out of County for about two weeks and in the rehab or domiciliary trying to learn how to live without being high or trying to be high.

"Hello?" I recognized that the number was from California and not Oklahoma, where my demons seemed to be residing.

"Hey Kid, what are you doing?"

I almost dropped the phone. It was my dad, Alan Mangini—my childhood hero who was always cooler than the Fonz.

"Oh hey, Dad, how are you?" My voice sounded so foreign and healthy.

"I am calling you. I heard you were doing well—"

The phone went dead.

I still do not know if I screamed or if it was in my head, but what I do know is that I ran down the hallway in my socks to where there was better reception. Once I slid to a stop, I called my father back.

"Did you hang up on me?!" His voice came across my cracked screen.

I quickly retorted with "No!"

He laughed and said he figured that the call dropped. He talked to me like it had not been years since we had last spoken with each other. Of course, the last conversation had been me asking for money and him telling me that would be the last time. Maybe it was when I was losing my house and he had said something like, "Are you a dumbass?" I had no reply then because I truly felt like I was the biggest fuck up on the planet at that time, and the only time I felt good was when I was so high I did not feel anything.

"I think going back to Oklahoma is a mistake and I told Kris you should move here, so we have a little house on the property that is yours if you want it."

Again, I almost dropped the phone. I looked out the large window at my reflection and the large American flag softly moving in the night breeze.

"I would love that," I said, "and thank you."

He said OK and continued to ramble, which is so not my dad. "Yeah, I am looking out my window now and I can see our cows—"

"Wait, you have cows?!"

"Of course!" He answered like we had always had farm animals and then added something to the effect that there were only 286 people in the town.

My heart sank. I mean, was there even a McDs? The answer: no.

But it would be the best move I ever made, back into the loving arms of my family.

AMC HORNET

Picture if you will a perfect family vacation, and you might see some pieces of that vacation in this story.

Cue the good-looking family: handsome dad, beautiful mom, one timeless beauty of a young teen girl, an adorable brother, and me.

So here we are in our family vehicle, a 1974 AMC HORNET, (as my mom will tell you, "the only brand new car she ever bought!") in a shade of green that only the early 1970's dreamt up. I am pretty sure it did not have A/C, and I think there was an AM/FM radio. We did not touch the seatbelts, and my brother and my favorite spots to sit were the "back-back" (under the hatchback).

I think Tony and I were about seven or eight, so this was maybe 1979ish. The family trip was from the Bay Area of California to Dallas, Texas, to visit family friends. If you have ever taken that trip across the states, usually I-40, you know that there is not a lot to look at, other than cactuses and the occasional truck stop. Today there is more, of course, because that is the way things go, and also, there is more to do in a vehicle. You can play games on your phone or watch movies on any device you choose. I am sure you can think of more ways to be engaged on a road trip.

We had two rules: Do not enter the back seat (because that was my older sister Tina's area) and no arguing.

Other than that, it was to play I-Spy, sing rounds of 99-bottles of soda (not beer), and hours of "I'm not touching you!" to pass the time. So, you can guess where I am going with this story.

Let me take a moment and tell you that when I was five years old, I had to get my tonsils removed and my gramma Dorothy had bought me a koala bear from the hospital gift shop. I loved my gramma more than anything and so, I loved this koala bear almost the same. I do not remember the exact details, but I am sure that bear had been in my life for a few years. I do have shadowed memories of being young and holding it when I was going to sleep, so I know it would have been "well loved" by the time we took this trip. (Meaning: it was a bit beat up.)

Anyway, Tony and I got into some sort of tiff and somehow the koala bear was suddenly between us. Voices escalated and then—!

The little black threads that made the mouth of my bear were no longer attached.

My anger was unmatched from anything I had ever known before and my brother was my target. My beloved koala bear became an extension of my arm as I attempted to beat my brother while crying and yelling in my eight-year-old voice.

At some point we became the attention of my dad, Mom, and older sister Tina, who was probably simply happy that she had the whole back seat to herself!

The small station wagon did not signal its intention to pull over. No, my dad expertly flung us off the boring and not crowded interstate highway to the hot sandy shoulder, and came to a halt. Dad turned off the engine. (I did not notice nor care, and come to think of it, Tony probably did not notice either since I was attempting to perform the first throat punch of my life.)

With ignition key in hand, Dad flung the driver's door open and took giant Dad steps to the back of the vehicle. Key was quickly inserted to unlock and open the hatch back, then the shadow of Mr. Mangini came across seconds before he reached in to pull us apart!

I honestly do not remember anything else, except maybe a cactus in the background behind his silhouette.

Dad, Jennifer, Tony, and Tina at Meteor Canyon, NM

Tony, Mom, Tina, and Jennifer at Meteor Canyon, NM

Tony, Tina, Jennifer, and Mom at Meteor Canyon, NM

Domino Effect

I remember playing dominoes with my brother and sister when I was a kid. We did not play the traditional game of calculating the dots on the dominoes; we played the game of setting them up in lines and knocking them over. We would weave them up and down the green linoleum in our kitchen, giggling with excitement while we set them up. I remember carefully crawling in between the strategically spaced-out paths, eager to see them all fall in the line. One of us gently knocked the first domino with hopefulness and excitement, watching as each domino fell into the next, finally laughing and celebrating when all the dominoes had collapsed along the path we had created. Little hands high-fived amongst the black and white blocks scattered across the green kitchen floor.

I think life is sometimes like that dominoes game... we start with hopefulness and innocence, thinking all we need to do is set up the path and everything will fall into place. Of course, some of us, sooner than others, learn that life does not work quite like that. We have loved ones die unexpectedly, relationships end, someone cheats, because life throws us curveballs and sometimes we are not ready. Sometimes it is just life, good things happen to bad people and we do not understand why, especially when sad things happen to good people, cancer takes over someone, or addiction changes or ends a life.

I've learned that when the results come the way I wanted, it is because I put the work in alongside the right attitude and support system. Graduating from Basic Training & nursing school are two notable examples. I was humble and open to learning the lessons by the leadership or instructors in both situations. Then, I stuck through, achieved tenacity and discipline, and grew to understand the importance of learning and reaching the finish line— sometimes forgetting how much time and work was put into the entire process.

Sometimes one choice leads to another, feeling and looking benign, but sometimes things start moving in a direction that wasn't intended and when we look up, it is entirely the furthest away from anywhere we would have thought to go. I did not end up in Oklahoma County Jail because I worked in the aftermath of the Oklahoma City Bombing Tragedy, but that was one of the first dominoes to fall in the line of PTSD and addiction.

Each of the doors shown hold 2-3 women, or men. When we would be locked down we would not leave our cell for days.

Recovery was not all unicorns and rainbows—far from that. It is scary, it is tiring, it is painful. Speckled throughout the shit there are moments of purity—moments of clarity, like, "Wow, this Peet's coffee is amazing" or "Oh, wow, did I just feel peacefulness?"

A typical cell block in the Oklahoma City Jail

In those moments, I began to understand that there was a life beyond the darkness, beyond the trauma that had engulfed my existence. Now, back to the recovery process.

"Ms. Mangini, we are sending you home." The team of sophisticated, classy therapists and mental health providers all looked at me with the same eyes of disappointment.

"Ummm, hello, have you not looked at my file and, ahem, me? I am pretty fucked up and need this. I NEED THIS!" (Duh, cue eyebrows raised and slight eye roll, fists beginning to curl, heart rate increasing).

"Yes, but you refuse to talk."

"Well, you are the therapist, do your job," I said.

"That's not how this works; you have to allow us in to be able to do our job."

"F-you. Wait, ugh, anger. I feel anger. All I know or can articulate: ANGER!!!!"

"Okay, so that is a start," the poised woman said with a kind smile, her counterparts following suit.

My internal voice said, "This is not going to be easy."

But wow, it has been so, so worth it.

Dark Thoughts

MST is an acronym for Military Sexual Trauma. Rape. Sexual assault. Sexual violence.

Basically, the culture of the military is such that this is so common that there is now a specific diagnosis. When I was at WTRP, I was the only woman there who was not there because of some horrific incident or instances of MST from the men who served alongside them while serving our country. What the fuck. There's something wrong with this!

Death is a funny thing, not ha-ha funny, but the kind of funny that keeps you awake on a Wednesday night, kinda just sneaks in your thoughts. I wonder why cancer is still such a thing. Why is it still a death sentence for so many. Why does it literally destroy so many people from the inside out. Why do some people hate life but live for so long, while other people—ones who wake up every day excited about who they can help, who wake up happy and grateful for a new day—are usually the ones who get told they have weeks to live? Weeks, days, minutes.

Is this dark? Yep. But sometimes I feel like this. Sometimes I'm just mad because so many wonderful, dear friends, both veterans and civilians, are gone. Cancer, overdose, accidents... ugh, at least the ying/yang of life allows the good and the bad.

Innocent Kindness

"I'm never gonna see you again, am I?"

His young eyes had a wisdom deep inside and a hint of truth that made my heart ache. It was a question I had never wanted to hear, especially from someone so young.

I did not have an answer, honestly. I did not know. All I knew was I wanted to be able to answer and not lie.

I had asked a favor from a friend and she had allowed me to crash at her place for a few days, but the time had passed and she said it was time to go. I finished putting my luggage in the back of my truck and walked back into the house to tell her thank you when my friend's son's voice stopped me in my tracks. He just stood there looking at me with a mix of concern and curiosity.

Looking back, I can't remember what I said. I only know that I can still see him standing there looking so kind and young. I could not leave fast enough. I did not want to let him be around such ugliness, such wrongness. I guess that was how I felt inside. I was so lost that I could not see that his mother would never have let me stay and he would not have enjoyed talking with me if the ugliness I felt was actually me.

Since we are having this heart-to-heart conversation, I would like to ask you something. Have you wondered why someone who seemed like they were going in the right direction, making the right choices, why that person would do something so stupid? Why, especially if that someone is a Registered Nurse, a highly qualified, decorated veteran, skilled in caring and well-known for her kindness and integrity? Known for being a hard worker, dedicated, honest, and funny? The one person people knew they could always rely on?

Why make THAT choice? Why? The honest answer? I do not know.

(Sorry, that was probably a letdown.)

This book isn't about all the right answers and the best advice. Nope. Like I said, this is just my story and I hope and pray that I am able to help people, maybe you, or maybe your child—anyone really—because I never thought I could be an addict. Ever. Oh, no, no. I was smarter than that.

I was better than that.

I knew better.

But see, (and I hope this comes across well because I am going to try to explain what I mean) addiction is not "I got high and it felt good." I mean, I did get high, and a lot of times, it felt good, but to understand, or I guess let me try to explain... we have to dive deeper. And to do that, I am going to take a little bit of a turn to the left—or right. Anyway, a turn.

So, let's say I was telling you a story of when I was young and learning how to ride a bicycle. One awesome story that my family knows well is the one where I barreled down a hill, across a paved parking lot, passing my dad. I was seven or so, maybe younger. I do not remember, but I remember the feel of the wind in my hair, the woosh of air in my ears, and hearing faintly, "Slow down!!"

So being the obedient daughter, I started pressing back on the pedal to brake. This did cause my bike to slow down, but my body did not. My front tire slid across gravel, but my back tire was stuck on the end of the pavement. I fell face first off the bike, flying across the dusty gravel and then came to a stop. My dad was there before I could react, and he was telling me how awesome I looked—probably told me I was like the legendary Evil Knievel— and he had me giggling by the time we got back home.

What I did not know was that one side of my face looked horrific, all bloody and torn up, still dirty and bleeding. I did realize this when my mom laid eyes on me and started crying and freaking out.

(But Jennifer, this is a book about addiction and bombing. Yes, I am getting there. It is gonna tie together.)

Dad had Mom and me freaking out, so he did what any normal man would do in the mid 1970's—he grabbed the Cannon camera and started taking pictures of my mom pouring peroxide on my face. (The real stuff that bubbled like it was going to fizz my face off!)

After the drama and the tears (mostly my mom's), I am thinking they gave me some children's Tylenol and some ice cream.

Normal. Kid. Stuff.

So, if I had broken my arm, they would have taken me to the hospital and I would have been given pain medicine. If I had woken up with a fever, I would have gotten pain medicine. And here is my point. It became natural for me to equate pain with the need for something to numb it. But wait, I digress! (I always wanted to write that in a book!) Anyway, this is a key point. I didn't even realize how much I needed help, needed an outlet, and did not see that the pain and loneliness was only caused by my shutting people out and myself in.

When I used drugs—even from the first time—it was to help make the pain disappear. It was to slow the critical voice that continually kept saying what a disappointment I was and what a failure I was. I mean, what kind of person makes the decision NOT to be there for her adorable little nephews and nieces? Who decides to live 2,000 miles away but still wakes up every day so incredibly lost and lonely? I will actually answer that question. It was me. The kind of person who feels immense guilt but masks it with substances to mute the chaos inside.

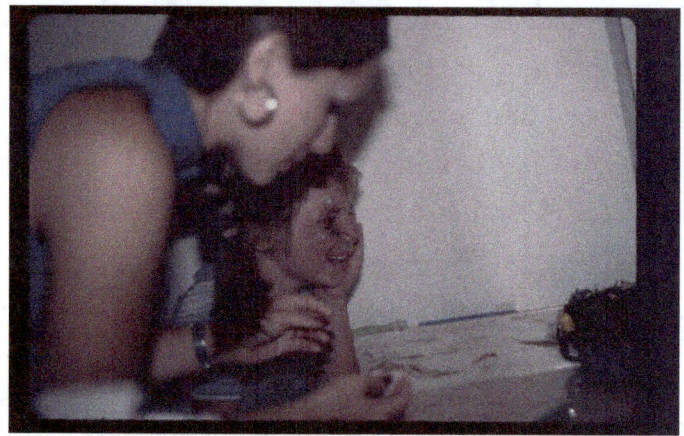

Jennifer with her mother

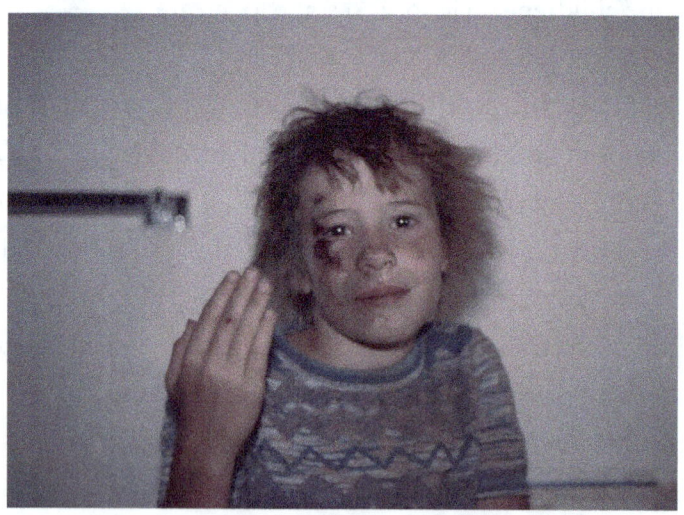

Jennifer with a bruised and scraped up face

Why was it so okay that we took a pill to make a physical ailment better but never consider that we as humans need help mentally?

I am so glad that society has changed where mental health is now talked about and it is so widely accepted that mental and physical health are absolutely essential to a person's life. But at that time, I felt trapped in a spiral, unable to reach out or get the help I needed. As the years went on, the weight of my unaddressed trauma and addiction grew heavier.

It is that pain that we feel when we lose the grandma who we love more than air. It is the pain of losing the best friend who never gets to grow up, the pain of losing a father who never made it past twenty-one, the pain of out-living a child.

That pain of never getting to be a parent.

Or the pain of that first love saying goodbye. Or being cheated on by someone you thought was forever (for real this time!).

Or maybe having to make the hard decision and letting that furry best friend companion cross over the rainbow bridge.

I do not know your pain. What I know is what I have felt and how debilitating and time-stopping a traumatic event can be, even if it is years later and it is 'only' a thought, a 'trigger,' a memory, a smell, a something that literally pulls you back through time.

That first time...

Tired beyond belief. Working nights and loud kids during the day (no blame - they were just kids), exhausting schedule and no end in sight. Life was tiresome and banal. I asked her if she could get me whatever it was that she had done to give her all that energy.

Her answer: "No, you do not." But while her words said no, her eyes sparkled with that sparkle that always made my knees weak. Along with the sparkle in those mesmerizing blue eyes, her full red lips had that tilted smirk that always got me in trouble.

"Yeah, I do," I said.

"Ok... Fuck ya."

I fell back into my bed. I am sure I was asleep (probably already about to snore and drool) before my head hit the pillow, reminiscent of when I was a toddler and would face-plant mashed potatoes as I fell asleep at dinner. Sometime later, I was awoken to her voice and the sound of the utility room door closing behind her.

"I'm not sober anymore!"

I came out of my slumber as she was coming into the bedroom with her smile lighting up her face.

"Wait til you try this," she said. "You're gonna feel great!"

Now, my background with substance use was extremely limited. I had smoked some weed in high school, but alcohol was more my JAM (btw those are also my initials and automatically scored me higher in cool points, at least in my mind. Okay, back to the subject).

Also note that I said I smoked weed. No, I did not pay attention if it was Kush or Stevia. Wait, that's fake sugar. Man it is hard to be old and still alive sometimes. Okay, Sativa, Hybrid, or Indica. I also did not have a cool bong or fancy lighter. No, my drug experience had been poking holes in a Pepsi can, removing seeds (they pop!) and smoking some weed before heading to 7-Eleven for delicious snacks and a lot of giggles.

All that being said, I was clearly the student and she was my coach to this newness. Of course, neither of us realized it would become my lifestyle even as later I heard someone harshly say, "They were witnessing the demise of Jennifer Mangini."

We do not know until we do.

I am gonna borrow a line from the movie 'Bolt' and "put a pin in that," meaning, I will address the demise and then *JENN2.0* later because I think this part is important. Please do not get me wrong, I am kinda having fun going back and storytelling. I hope you are enjoying the read; there is more here though. If you do not know how it feels and what life is like stuck in the chaos of addiction, my **hope** is you never will. Because what I did not fathom was that I ever would, or even could, because I was not like "those people." What I am telling you is, I absolutely was, and just could not believe it or see it-and this is why I am being so transparent and honest. Maybe I can help someone... maybe someone you know or maybe even you.

I am not sure if you have noticed this about me, or recognize any traits we may share, but I like to excel. I love to win, to be the best, to know that when I have done something or anything, that I have put in 1000%. That being said, sometimes giving something your 'everything' takes more than you can ever imagine. So where were we...

"Ok, you inhale when I say so," she said. "Oh, and inhale it in all the way down to your toes and then hold your breath—that makes it work better!"

I nodded slightly in acknowledgment, sluggishly sleepy and eyes barely open from the abundance of melatonin raging through my body.

She lit the glass bowl, twisting side to side, and then said, "Ok, now!"

I inhaled slowly, deeply, and then even deeper, because remember, if I am going to do something, I am going to DO IT.

When I first inhaled and then exhaled the billow of white smoke, the physical sensation was so intense, it made my brain stop thinking. My anxiety exploded—the darkness shrouding my being dissipated, the ache slipped out of my bones, the melatonin quickly being replaced by a rush of manufactured dopamine.

The outside of my legs, from right above my ankles, started tingling, and this flow of aaaahhhhhhhh just encompassed my whole being. The world shifted, colors became brighter, and the weight of everything lifted from my shoulders. I was awake for what felt like the first time in my life, and

I felt like I was home. It was reminiscent of when I was walking into our house as a child from riding in the 1974 AMC HORNET with the windows down (hot air instead of a/c) and into the invigorating, wonderful, magnificent electric AIR CONDITIONING!

I felt like I was home, like I finally belonged somewhere. Okay, so now what?

UNICORNS AND RAINBOWS, Y'ALL!

Today.

Today my life is full.

Full of love, happiness, and joy. It is all unicorns and rainbows.

Wait, no it is not. It is... life. My beautiful wife, Laurie, and I live a busy and fun life. I have an incredible large family and support system who are some of the most amazing people I know. I wake up most days with my heart so full because there are blessings that I could not have ever dreamed of. We live in the Pacific Northwest (PNW) and have two rescue dogs. We focus on living our best life.

On another note, my lower back, knees, and both feet take turns aching while my tinnitus (all leftover gifts from the military) is so fucking high-pitched and loud.

Ugh, or rather, EEEEEEEEEEEEEEEEEEEEEE.

(You thought I was going to stay with unicorns and rainbows? Pfft, life is messier than that).

Yes. It is a nice, simple, no-drama life. It is exactly what I've wanted; it is what I dreamed for, begged God for, fell to my knees (not literally but in my mind) in south OKC for on one snowy spring night, sick with pneumonia, broke and so broken, not high, and definitely not enjoying life. That night was the last night I was on the street and the first time I was so completely tired and exhausted, too exhausted to even care about hating the person I was. I just could not keep living this life. God knew, and the universe opened up with a plan.

Funny how these plans go; they are never what we expected, thought, or wanted, but they are exactly what we need.

Hello, smelly OKLAHOMA COUNTY JAIL.

Ugh, so when going through changes in life, I bet you are like me in that I do not always like the journey of the change being implemented.

Let me explain. I had a plan that morning—a plan for tacos, delicious, crispy, greasy tacos from the local taco mayo, but alas, no money. So, with sidekick running buddy, Josh, and a youngster chick that was wanting to—I do not know, maybe get with Josh, or just bored and wanted to do something different—we went to figure out how to score a lick, making some quick money for tacos and dope. Josh and I had been runnin' buddies for a fat minute. We knew each other and worked well together, communicating without words, at least until we were celebrating and smokin', usually cracking stupid jokes. This would not be the case, and sadly, there were no tacos.

My brother, Tony, called me one day about a year ago and said he had a dream. Now, usually when we talk about a dream, it entails something about being a superhero, or cool shit like that, or something totally stupid that we laugh like eight-year-olds over. This was very different, and he had a request. He wanted me to paint my interpretation of the dream he described. I was intrigued and quite honored.

Now, I would like to say I wrote out what he told me that day, so I would be able to go back and have written words to rely on instead of my memory, but I did not. Here is what I recall: it was a dream of me holding a cookie sheet, silver and clean, but then with rust and scratches throughout, kinda warped, very used. I go to show it to him, maybe hand it to him, and as he grabs it, the metal changes form, wrapping around his hand and forearm, clasping around, and hurting his hand. He starts laughing though as we try to remove it and then beautiful pieces start falling off, making something shiny and more beautiful than the original metal sheet. Tony then told me he thought of it as me. I had become hurt and broken, but now as I started healing, the person I was becoming was so beautiful, and he was so proud of me... proud to be my brother. We both cried. I added that I saw in the description of his dream, that when the metal wrapped around his hand and arm, causing pain, and cutting him, blood dripping down, that was how much I had hurt him with my struggles, when I isolated myself.

I cannot write this without tears, honestly. It is my opinion that the pain I caused is far worse than the pain I felt while in the depths of addiction, mainly because I got to be numb. I was able to stay unaware, or pretend to be anyway, always focusing only on me and all my problems.

Okay, now that I have gotten up and grabbed my Kleenex, let's get back to my artistic interpretation of Tony's dream. There is a woman, like a female warrior standing atop the large silver area (picture a large shiny lake), and beneath that is a large blue area (same lake only very deep and blue), which feels strong yet so peaceful and warm with love. There is a colorful swirl of activity nearby—blues, purples, grays, and golds, whirling in loud, chaotic energy that you can almost feel. Full of sadness, fear (like the frozen, scared to death kind), and sheer rage and anger. The anger isn't towards anyone; it is internal somehow. There is a sense of calm as you look deep into the blue. It is intense while it almost feels like the surface is just that—a surface. And if you scratched it, you could get inside and be safe and loved. Above the woman are spatters of pastels—sherbet—and softness, encompassing the softness of the best pillow you could ever imagine, only in colors on a canvas. My take on the interpretation? I am glad you asked! I feel like that dream helped us understand each other and grow so incredibly close. I, like most, would never have chosen to hurt myself, or my family, the people who loved me and were helpless to help, while I was so angry no one was there for me.

Jenn's interpretation of Tony's dream

Jenn and Tony at Heather Farm Pool, Walnut Creek, CA, circa 1978

TALENT COMES AS A SURPRISE

I did not know I could paint until I got into recovery. I discovered a hidden talent I never knew I had. Expressing myself through art became my therapy, my refuge from the chaos. It is interesting to see what kind of art comes out when it is done in a therapeutic way. Let me try to explain what I mean.

Maybe you are someone who thinks, "Today I will channel my inner Bob Ross and create a perfect image of _____ (insert subject)."

When (and please remember, I am only speaking from MY mind and experience, and I am not usually the 'norm') I go to create art, I have zero luck painting or drawing or creating what I set out to create. It goes like this: blank canvas leaning on my wooden easel + assortment of brushes + a thought of what I want to paint. Let's say a dog.

Yes, there is no dog in this picture. Nothing that even comes close to those four-legged furry friends of ours! This bothered me when I was young and simply had decided that I had zero talent in the art department. My biological father had been an extremely talented artist, and I just gave up, because I figured that gene just did not make it to me.

Like I said above, I only discovered that I did actually have a good bit of talent, it was just not the norm. One of my favorite parts of my art is that people always find different things in my paintings, and I actually am sometimes amazed at what I know I just painted—without realizing that there was anything distinguishable on the canvas until I stepped back. My mom, for example, always sees birds; many have told me they see different faces and I even had one friend in Kansas who always seemed to see boobies in my art! All silliness aside, I have seen a change in my art while in the recovery journey. When I started and was still so full of anger that I could not see any future, I had to trust the men and women who told me there was hope, and there was a way out of the darkness. All I had to do was focus on one step, one day, one 24-hour period, sometimes even having to break it down to just that single moment. Then take the next step, shaky and scared but determined not to go backwards or become stagnant. Those early canvases follow the same trends—darkness, scribbles—almost scratched into the canvas. The feeling of dismay, confusion, and anger.

CHA-CHA-CHANGES

April 19, 2025.

Now this is my time. Fuck yeah!!! (Sorry, Mom.)

Side note: My mom is an author and I love her books. She witnesses her Christian faith through incredible stories and I recommend her as an author: Joan Bannan! She believes in writing without swearing. I literally do not know how to do life without swearing, but I totally respect her. Like I already said, I love her books. So on to the awesomeness of returning to the life of a nurse. Omg. Wait. WHAT!!!!

R.N. REGISTERED NURSE!!!

I worked in bedside patient care from 1993 to 2014 in some capacity, from the beginning when I was a medical technician in the Army, Combat Medic outside the hospital setting. Born to kill, trained to save—oh wait, this is a more serious section.

I have stayed long after my shift ended to sit with a dying patient whose family members did not show up, just so they would not leave this life alone. I never understood how a family could know that an individual was dying but not care enough to be there for the last breath. Of course, sadly, I know sometimes they only cared about the monthly money coming in from their "loved one." Do I sound bitter? Well, sorry. Not sorry. I have cried in the bathroom after a patient died, more than once, I feel it is a calling to be a nurse. In my opinion, it is an honor to be a nurse, even though sometimes after a hard shift or a patient is being rude just to be rude, I can think maybe I should be doing something else. When I wake up the next morning, however, I know I am doing what I am supposed to do when I walk onto the unit, especially at the VA, with my fellow veterans.

It is so hard to live without honesty and integrity. I enjoy living on this side where, yeah, life is life, but I am open, honest, and just me.

LIFE IN THE STREETS

Here are some of the 'rules' I learned: Walk all night because if you stay still, it is not safe. Look for money-making opportunities anywhere and everywhere, and when you still have not figured out how to put some cash in your pocket, look for change under the drive through windows. Look for anything that might have copper or that can be traded later during normal business hours. If you find that you need to sleep, make sure it is somewhere that you can hide your backpack so you still have it in the morning. This can be difficult and many times, I would end up couch surfing various apartments or people's homes around the city.

One weekend, I was staying with a friend who rented a room in an older trailer. It was only heated by the ceramic heater I had brought (probably why I ended up staying a couple months now that I think of it) and had so many roaches living there that we never turned all the lights off in the bedroom. Food was always an integral daily part of the plan. If I had food available, I could focus on pullin' a lick (making money) or maybe going and reupping, which was always the goal of every day. I mean, a person would want to be high in order to stay in a place that makes Joes apartment look clean!

So, this particular weekend, my friend and I had a three-pound bag of dried cranberries, a large jar of sweet pickle relish, and a few boxes of Triscuits. It was snowing so even if we did have money, we did not want to risk the two-mile hike through the woods to the dollar store. On a good note, relish and crackers is not a bad snack. I would not suggest three days of it though.

9:01/9:02

9:02

What do you think when you see the time above? I see it and my heart skips. Reality stops and I am suddenly in the Alfred P. Murrah building, a witness to that sad tragedy.

9:01.

TICK.

My mind's eye sees a sharp dressed woman setting a Pyrex container full of brownies on the break room table, her perfectly manicured nails in a fancy French tip that her sister had talked her into getting before dinner at Denny's the evening before.

TICK.

I see a young mother walking her toddler into the daycare, anxious to get upstairs and get ready for a mid-morning meeting with her new boss.

TICK.

Two twin boys laughing and giggling together at the daycare window as their favorite daycare worker puts out the first of the mid-morning snacks—graham crackers and fruit are sure to be a hit.

TICK.

A Marine hurriedly pouring hazelnut creamer into his coffee cup, watching the break room door for anyone because he has always told everyone how real Marines only drink black coffee. (But dang the creamer makes the coffee so tasty!)

TICK.

An executive businessman, still having a strong linebacker physique from his college days, strolling through the lobby and smiling at that cute blonde receptionist checking him out as he walked by. He certainly always checked her

TOCK.

9:02.

GROWTH AND BOOBIES

I learned a while back to really pay attention to the words I say or think, because each word carries energy and meaning. This can be awesome and helpful: "I am grateful and blessed!"

This phrase is one I say so much and I love it. Sometimes, I am not feeling all unicorns and rainbows, and instead of following the easy path towards negativity, those five words remind me I am so incredibly grateful and blessed.

I worked hard to eliminate words like hate, or anything that could draw negativity towards me. These efforts transformed my mindset, helping me to focus on the blessings scattered throughout my day-to-day life, no matter how small.

That's the thing about good times. Sometimes you realize their effective way after the fact.

"Dig deeper."

Ugh. I was not even trying to make my face not show my annoyance. The sun shining outside the Menlo Park building was beautiful and bright, a small jet-black squirrel ran across the lawn, perfectly in rhythm with the leaves riding the soft breeze.

"What do you feel?" she asked, pulling my attention back to the group.

Man her job would suck, always having to get people to talk, I thought, unsure how to put the constant swirling chaos inside into words.

"Irritated," I said. "And confused." I couldn't understand why the information seemed just out of reach, elusive and infuriating. "Pissed off. Annoyed."

"Deeper," she said.

My arms were crossed and I was shaking my leg. The other women sat patiently; they were pretty used to this dance between the therapist and Jennifer.

"Oh my freaking—Really irritated!"

"Okay, look at the wheel and find an emotion—"

"I hate your stupid wheel." My brain's voice started the normal negative tirade, but today I stopped it. I took a deep breath and forced my eyes back to the colorful wheel. "Maybe frustration," I said suddenly, a little more forcefully than I meant.

Breathing slowly, I forced myself to focus, hoping clarity would eventually emerge from the tangled web of thoughts. "Guilt. Shame."

"And beneath that?" she probed gently, her eyes meeting mine with unwavering patience.

"Sadness."

For some reason, the normal feeling of not wanting to talk, especially in front of anyone, even if I had already heard how fucked up they were, was not present. No, quite the opposite actually! These words started rolling out like cars on a roller coaster going downhill. It surprised me how effortlessly they flowed, spilling words and emotions I didn't even realize I held.

"That's good. That is what we are trying to find—the emotion underlying the anger."

She smiled kindly and just for a moment, I had hope. Hope, a faint glimmer, began to crack through the thick, darkened walls I'd built, wanting to keep people out, but unintentionally trapping me inside.

***

Sometimes, life is moving along and everything seems more gray, more muddled, and harder to see the good and bad until after the fact. Here is one of those circumstances:

"You better not boob punch me!"

"Oh yeah!?"

"Yeah!"

We sounded like we were a couple of ten-year-old girls. Of course, I took the adult action and—Smack!

(Did you really think I was going to do the adult thing? That would be so boring!)

Christal jumped up and the WTRP (woman's trauma and recovery program) VA therapist looked over at us—more than slightly annoyed.

"Hey!! I am so mad! She punched me in the boob!" she yelled, basically snitching on me.

I retorted, "I barely touched her and if I had actually boob-punched her, she would be crying for real!"

We were sent to the therapist's office... well, the 'therapists' as in the trio of well-trained, well-dressed, and well, annoyed, professional women. This was not the first time we had been ordered to the figurative principal's office. It would be the last time, however, that we would be there for this reason.

The lead therapist looked up, sighed and rubbed her face exasperatedly with her hands.

Then she looked down at each of us like a headmaster of a very disciplined university. Again, with a disappointed sigh, she asked, "What are we supposed to do with this? Fighting? Really? You two ladies are grown adults and—"

"Christal," I interrupted, turning my seated body towards her, looking at her face, into her hazel, or actually, really, really green eyes (they only turned that color when she was terribly angry). This was the beginning of what was sure to be an extraordinarily long, drawn-out (one-sided) conversation. Christal had already been allowed to tell her side, which was surprisingly accurate and also probably smart on the therapists' end so that they were able to hear the more forthcoming version from Christal and not the extremely limited version from me. Remember, I do not like to share information.

With my face full of sincerity, more than I had shown to anyone in an exceptionally long time, open and honest feelings shown in my deep brown eyes, I said, "I apologize."

The three therapists, Christal, and honestly, internally myself, looked at me with astonishment. Mouths dropped open in shock.

"You asked me not to boob punch you and I did not listen; I am sorry and it will not happen again," I added.

Silence. Total silence. I do not think the three women took a breath, and then, "Thank you. I accept your apology," my roommate in the program said... this pink sock-wearing, Navy veteran, and downright badass woman.

I do not remember all of what happened next, but I do know that something in me had returned. I was once again someone who took responsibility for my actions. I was ready to heal. I wanted this person as my friend and it hurt my heart to see that I caused her pain, not just physically but mentally. I woke up to who I was— someone who protects and supports my people.

Christal and a puppy in Menlo Park VA, 2017

Trigger Alert

When I was in the Army, our boots were black. They were like their own brand, if you will. Stick with me here; this is just some random thoughts I am having and it is literally the middle of the night.

Okay, so boots. Jump boots, tanker boots... (Enter the chorus of "These boots are made for walking." Just kidding, we marched!

Okay, focus. Army boots. I did not realize until recently that today's Army boots are not black and not at all shined, which I think is kinda weird and almost disappointing. I remember learning how to shine my boots, just the right ratio of spit and black polish, with just the right amount of pressure, small circles using an extra brown undershirt because it was the softest material. Some people had the ability to make it look like they did nothing and suddenly those boots shined like the sun!

My battle buddy, Rachel, and I got pretty good at shining our boots, and we had a lot of hours together, sometimes laughing and sometimes tired as hell. But dang, our boots shined! Of course, the boots also got really dirty really fast, sometimes because we were young and thought it would be awesome to 'hawk a loogie' onto the other person's boot right before inspection (which made that person have to do pushups!) and sometimes because of our hard work in bad situations.

Fast forward to the day I looked down and had brain matter on my boot. I unzipped the body bag, and like something out of a horror movie, fluids and brain matter dripped and splat onto my black Army boot. I looked down in stunned horror and could not unsee the grey clumps on the now not-so-shiny surface.

Could I have just cleaned the boot? Yes. Did I want to? No.

I do not want to get too graphic, because I want to honor the memory of the men, women, and children who died senselessly in this horrific attack. That being said, I had assisted in helping identify a person who could only be identified by dental records, their body destroyed to know what they looked like in life. I stood awkwardly in the back of the closed refrigerated semi-truck trailer, straddling the body of the slain United States Marine, holding the flashlight for the dentist to visualize and compare the molar and the other once-white teeth inside the mouth of the Marine. His neck was so obscenely cracked and broken that a single person could not complete the needed tasks of opening the mouth and supporting the head at the same time. Scenes occupy space in my brain like old Polaroids in the back of a drawer, always there when I am looking for something else, and inevitably stop time, rudely slamming me back into that coroner's building in 1995.

We had a debriefing every day at the end of our shift at the Southwestern Bell building which was up the street from the federal building (now ground zero aka the bombing site). The Southwestern Bell building had become the hub for us and other government agencies to use and operate out of, as well as the US Post Office building nearby because of the proximity and locations.

So, I go to where I'm supposed to talk about my feelings (which, as a young, strong soldier and someone who was always taught to suck it up, don't cry, and shake it off),and my answer was usually one word. Fine. I was far from it, but I was not aware of it or maybe better said, I did not know how to articulate or explain anything. Besides, I was in soldier mode. Also, I was in the uniform I had been wearing for the long shift, picking up and through the victims. I mean, I already told you that death smells different, and this horror brought the worst out in those people.

Sitting in a circle, all of us smelly and physically, mentally, and emotionally exhausted, we said as little as possible so we could get out of there and decompress ourselves with hot showers and alcohol... at least that's what I did. Before we could leave, I glanced down at my boot.

It was not shiny. It was black leather, but there was gray matter all over my left boot. I froze. My breath caught in my throat, a mix of horror and disbelief. The others on my team followed my gaze at my boot, because maybe I was saying my one-word answer of 'fine,' or maybe I gasped, I do not know.

Whoever was in charge said, "Hey Mangini, they have a makeshift PX at the post office. Why don't you walk over and grab some new boots?"

I nodded in agreement, which was not like me, but as you already know, this was not a normal situation. I walked outside onto the sidewalk and there was a cyclone fence that had been erected quickly to prevent people from entering the area around the bombing site and the now-famous building that I also cannot NOT see in my own mind. There was somebody's daughter standing there looking at the site, her small hands raised above her head, holding the fence, her forehead pressed against the metal wires. Such innocence and such horror—my mind did not want to compute. I walked past her and past the site, large and disgustingly imposing. There was a short line to enter the PX, so I took my place in line, trying not to look down at my boot. A woman came up behind me and took her place in line. I felt her presence before I turned and saw her. She seemed out of place—an island of calm amidst the chaos. When our eyes met, we said hello to each other, and she told me she was a minister at a local church.

This was 1995. I had never heard of a woman minister, let alone spoken with one! We had a short conversation, partly because the line moved quickly and partly because when I turned around to talk to her, all of the canvas behind her was the broken building. If she said her name, it would have been lost in my brain, but the feeling I had while speaking with her was simply the love and gratitude she gave me at that moment.

I tried to find her later, even going old school by pulling out the yellow pages and calling every church in the area. Not one said there were female ministers. In fact, a few actually laughed at my insistence a woman held that role. I will probably never know for sure, but I like to think that I spoke to an angel that day. Maybe she was or perhaps she was just a human being who helped me in an extremely difficult situation.

Support in a Different Way

Two different size big toes... I can't make this stuff up. Seriously. It's like a comedy sketch come to life. I look down in disbelief or maybe awe, no, maybe sadness. You know, I am not sure if it is sadness, so that is not coming out right.

Let me explain from the beginning. This is real life—my life. And my not-so-big toe. Did I mention it is not the same size as the other one? Well dang, I guess I did. Crazy, right?

Foot surgeries, as in not just one... Actually, not even two, because that would be somewhat logical. I mean, two feet, one surgery each. No. I have had a total of four, two for each foot. Remember when I said I ran and marched in those combat boots while in the Army? Apparently, a woman running in flight or wearing stiff leather combat boots made for men and not meant for running in, is prone to damage her feet in so many ways it is not even funny. I guess the funny-not funny part of this is feeling a ripping sensation in my foot, either along the plantar area or the arch. It would hurt like hell, in a very 'wrong feeling' way, and I would try to walk it off or if it were the end of the day, I would take off my boots, shine the top with my sweaty sock and then massage my achy arches. I thought it was something everyone went through and just kept my mouth shut, because no one wanted to be "that person." Karens were just people we knew, not a whole symbol of someone complaining about the manager. Little did I know that the ripping sensation was not normal, and my arches would flatten causing my feet to grow two sizes over the next ten years, causing me so many issues including a lot of pain!

Yes, there is that, but let's go even further back.

Tony, Tina, and Jennifer circa mid 1970's

Size Matters

Actually, I am going to go back just a bit further to when I was around eleven years old.

I had a growth spurt and grew a few inches taller, mainly because my lower extremities had stretched seemingly overnight. My pants were now more like ill-fitting capris and my feet were even more narrow with my toes smashed at the end of my shoes. My wonderful Grandma Dorothy (Grama) took me to buy shoes at the downtown Emporium Capwell because she wanted to have 'someone who knew what they were doing' to measure my feet. I was excited because she was my favorite person and any time with her was always so wonderfully special. Also, we were the only ones going, just me and her; I could hardly contain myself!

Past the racks of expensive pretty blouses and pants hung lengthwise on velvety hangers, just adjacent to the lady's makeup and perfume counters, with the smiling but sometimes bored looking men who wanted to spray perfume on us (Grama said No!), we finally were at the ladies' shoe counter. Of course, there were racks of high heels and other shiny pretty shoes ready to be picked out, but first, the measuring would occur! The nicely dressed salesman nodded yes to Grama's request and winked at me as he politely said, "You ladies can sit at the first red vinyl bench."

Sitting down where he had gestured, I quickly removed my uncomfortable shoes and spied the wondrous shiny steel metal device. It had an outline of a foot and there were lines for each inch indicating the shoe size, depending on where the end of the aforementioned foot's toes went. He knelt on one knee and said to place my heel where the foot diagram showed the heel. When I had my heel in place, I stood and peered down to see the size.

One quick side note... I know I keep saying this, but there are so many differences between the 'then and now,' and one such fact was that women did not have large feet. In fact, shoes only went to size ten then and usually those shoes were nothing any woman would want to wear.

Everyone (and I mean everyone!) wore the average sized six, seven, or eight. Maybe a few wore a smaller size five, but NO ONE wore bigger than an eight. Okay, back to it... and I bet you are already guessing—

My brown eyes saw my toes pass those normal marks, past size seven... eight... eight and a half... and then nine. NINE.

The salesman glanced up and said, "Look straight ahead so we get the right size!" Panicked and feeling the tense air surrounding us, I looked across the shiny white flooring at the horizon of black business men's shoes on the display racks. "Wow! How old is this young lady?" he asked my grandmother, with a slight undertone of a chuckle.

"Eleven," Grama answered with a smile which quickly disappeared.

"Wow! You better hope she quits growing or she will have some huge feet!"

The next moments, as I recall, were a blur of activity. I am not sure if she told me to put my shoes on or if she just shoved them on, but either way, my same not-fitting uncomfortable shoes were back on my feet. Soon we were holding hands—well, she was gripping my hand and pulling me as fast as my almost-teen giraffe legs would carry me. Grama talked about how she didn't appreciate the gentleman's comment about HER granddaughter! I think we were outside the building before my brain realized she just stood up for me and that I would not be getting any shoes from that store. In fact, I do not remember ever going back to that store with her, and knowing her, she probably never did.

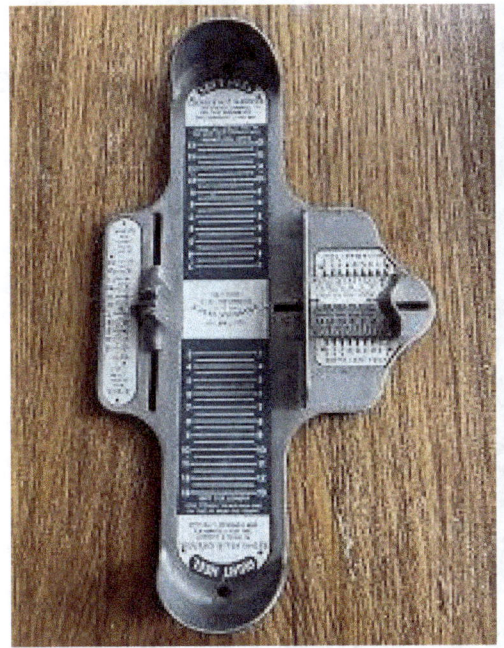

The measuring device for feet in the 1970's

My beautiful 'Grama' Dorothy

Bobble Heads and Bob Marley

I walked into the sprawling pink building with a bit of trepidation. My friend JoJo had gotten a job at the VA and said there was this cool lady who had helped her. My goal was to work at the VA as a nurse and be able to help veterans like I had been helped! As I stepped inside, the familiar hum of bustling activity surrounded me, reminding me of the many stories and lives intersecting here. Still, I had guards up because that's what I do.

"Hello! It's so nice to meet you!" Eyes full of life and kindness combined with her smile melted my guard away in an instant. I followed her back through the building and into a small office, which seemed stuffed full of San Francisco Giants bobbleheads, and a large, mounted poster of Bob Marley. "What can I help you with? I hear you are a nurse?"

"I can't work as a nurse right now," I said, "because I didn't keep my license current when I lost my home. And then I got caught up in addiction. I don't know if they will let me be a nurse again."

Our conversation continued for almost an hour, sometimes with us laughing like we had been friends for years and sometimes with her scribbling notes on who she knew or who she wanted to contact for me.

When I left the pink building that day, I felt different. I felt like she saw me as a nurse, and I knew she would do anything to help me. As I walked down the sunlit path away from the pink building, I felt a renewed sense of determination and hope. I had the right move to take the next steps toward reclaiming my career.

The world seemed brighter, possibilities expanded before me, and the echoes of our conversation replayed in my head, each word a step forward.

Priscilla worked for over forty years helping people get jobs in the Bay Area. Her dedication and compassion had changed countless lives, and now, it seemed, mine was next. As days turned into weeks, I found myself surrounded by opportunities I hadn't believed possible.

Of course, as life goes, many of the opportunities did not go as I expected. Most were just not the right fit, and one was close but then they looked at my background and decided I was not who they wanted. Eventually though, I was offered a job at the Palo Alto VA, not as a nurse yet (licensing was still not finalized and would not be completed for years), but as a healthcare professional—a Lead MSA or medical support assistant. An MSA was kinda like the old school ward clerk, working with the RN and on the team to help the veterans. I would be in a leadership role, and it sounded pretty fun! It wasn't exactly the position I dreamed of, but it was a step in the right direction. Grateful for the opportunity, I threw myself into my new role with enthusiasm, eager to make a difference. I was also excited that landing a job at the VA meant Priscilla would still collaborate with me to get me my RN back. I felt like the luckiest person ever!

Priscilla worked with the CWT program in Menlo Park, which helps veterans come back into the workforce, often from addiction and homelessness. She became my case worker and also a dear friend. Many times she kept me moving forward in my goal to not only work at the VA, but to work as an RN at the VA. There were years of many roadblocks and obstacles, and of course my PTSD, and the Taurus middle-child stubborn brain that would decide this was too hard. Priscilla would say, "Let's just make the phone call," or "Here, I wrote the letter for you. You can just review and sign it."

She was relentless in her support and encouragement. Sometimes, I wondered how she saw so much potential in me, especially when I was so disappointed in myself.

We met every thirty days in order for her to continue as my caseworker, and more than once, she would call and say, "I am driving to you. See you in about fifteen minutes!" This was huge because she was literally on the other side of the bay. Traffic there is a huge factor, so no one pops by, except Priscilla when she was showing up for a 30-day meetup!

Between the two of us working (and my incredible support system of course), I started working at the VA in 2020, not yet as a nurse but within the in-patient setting. This was good for me, because I saw that the RN role was within reach... it wasn't just something I had been and lost.

I would love to say it was overnight that I was able to become a licensed RN again, but of course, you already know life doesn't work like that. It was almost four years later that I won. Priscilla knew I had been granted the licensure but unfortunately, she lost a long battle to cancer in 2023. She didn't get to see me go to work as a nurse and I miss my friend every day. She was truly one of a kind. Her belief in me never wavered, not even in her final moments.

My life is so full and blessed! I was with my wife Laurie, my stepson Rick, and his friend, Joey, when the four of us had flown to Southern California for a weekend vacay. The guys were going to Disneyland and we were going to go find a spa or something fun. We all flew down and had great conversations and so much laughter!

Laurie and I dropped Rick and Joey off at the front of the iconic amusement park and started to pull off, looking to have our own little adventure when we saw the Guardians of the Galaxy ride towering in the sky. We were craning our necks to see the top of the ride (well I was, I think she could see it ok from her angle).

It was like a moment in a movie where two people had the same idea and the big lightbulb turned on above their head.

"We're going to Disneyland!" We said together to each other and giggled like two kids. After parking and getting our tickets, we called Rick and let him know that we were spending the day at the park, he laughed with his wonderful contagious laugh and we made plans where we would connect later that day.

It was a wonderful day, except at one point my feet were hurting so badly, we went to sit down and some dude made eye contact with me, started talking to me about how we could get some cut-the-line times for free and then, suddenly we were sitting in a time share meeting, with Laurie side eyeing me that look that said we would not be making a purchase today. I gave her the look back like of course not babe, half smile-and then. Beautiful resorts all over the world, Disney characters and luxurious luxury beckoned oozing with fun and charm. I almost said yes, probably would have if I had been alone, thank the Lord above for my beautiful rational wife, Laurie! She and I swore we would totally be in a better position to make that purchase later in life and practically ran out the door. Laughing and living in the moment of childlike wonder, we traversed the Magic Kingdom, walked around the shops, and met up with Rick and Joey, worn out and elated from the adventures. Of course, we were not finished and had a fabulous time riding Space Mountain, walking through the Star Wars land and of course the Guardians of the Galaxy ride was amazing!

COCKADOODLEDOO

The words wanting to make up this book wake me up quite demandingly so early in the morning, not as annoying as a dog barking or a rooster crowing, however, not as alluring as my lover inquiring with a suggestive voice if I am awake. It is akin to one of those waking lights, sometimes so softly and gently turning up until consciousness becomes my reality and words are flowing (along with the ever-constant noise of tinnitus).

The stream of energy, thoughts, and stories beg me to pick one and tell you, my dear reader friend, whatever the theme is of the day. Will it be one like the other morning, which had my heart open and vulnerable, tears flowing as I thought of how far I have come from my worst Christmas? It woke me and there was a persistent feeling of "write me, open me, share me" like a lump of coal in a pretty package.

Will it remind me of mornings when my friend let me sleep in the backyard of the men's sober house on the small cot hidden in the bushes? I say sleep but sleep was minimal because if anyone saw me, my friend would be kicked out and some of the other men living there were always a possible threat to my well-being. Either way, it was not the best situation but it was hidden and somewhat warm. My backpack and I, along with my shoes, stayed hidden and warm until the morning hours where it was still dark outside. And when the dew of dawn spread its coolness around or the cold, icy air threatened to freeze me, I'd climb out of the sleeping bag and sneak away, walking nowhere, and wiping sleep from my eyes.

Or will the words wake me with a funny moment, having me giggle under my breath (trying not to wake Laurie) and trying not to disturb the dog, who will wake with an adorable dog smile and promptly want to eat? Yes, I try not to, but somehow it will happen, or my minutes will tick away until my obnoxious alarm goes off, causing me to swear and the stream of words will vanish, so I quickly write.

I remember the fear, the icy coldness of the witching hour, the loneliness and never truly being safe, as I figured out the closest place to go brush my teeth and clean up. All this while I now lay in my incredibly awesome, comfortable bed, with 'my' pillow (if you have a bed mate you know how pillows are somehow switched and neither sleep well!). I lay on my grounding bottom sheet and my oh so perfectly soft mattress, my blankets that are clean and so inviting at the conclusion of my day.

Who's Salty? Not Me!

I shook the salt from the shaker into my hand. I was hungry and pretty excited about the meal in front of me. I had only been at the Domiciliary a short time and the bacon, scrambled eggs, and biscuits on my plate were like presents from the gods. However, they needed seasoning—salt and pepper to be exact—and that brought the conundrum. I was over forty and had abused my body for the last five or so years to the extent that things were not working as well anymore, i.e., I could not see the salt as it left the normal cafeteria-looking salt shaker and added flavor to my institutional scrambled eggs. This caused my eggs to be either extra salty or bland, and please, does anyone actually like bland eggs? (If you do, awesome. I am not judging. However, I like flavor and do not have any issues with my heart or fluid retention, so salt it up!) Like my dad says, "Salt is a preservative. Don't you want me around for a long time?"

Back to my inviting, yet unseasoned eggs... I could see the pepper as I shook the shaker, because pepper is black, but dang if the salt did not stay just out of my eyesight.

My work around was shaking salt into my left palm until I could see it, then setting the shaker down so that I could pinch the salt out of my palm and spread it across the plate, then wipe my hands to the side before commencing to eat my now-seasoned breakfast.

I don't know if you are like me and sometimes think you exist in a bubble where you can just meander away and people do not notice you. I mean, I know there are people who get in their cars and think somehow the glass must be tinted so well that no one can see them picking or digging for gold in their nostrils (yes, we can see you and yes, that is gross.).

This being said, apparently, I had performed my ritual of salting my food at every meal, not just breakfast, and people had noticed. In fact, the combination of me being a bit socially awkward, a bit shy sometimes, and this salt-pinching ritual caused more than one person to think I was snooty.

I'm sorry, what? Me, the person who once traded her "I found it so it's mine" bicycle for a shower? Me? Oh, you gotta be kidding me.

I found this out when I finally worked up the nerve to go play bingo one snowy Saturday (in the cafeteria where my snooty salt-pinching had been taking place).

There were a few people I recognized from one of my mandatory classes who waved me over and scooted down the metal bench for me to sit down. We had a few minutes to reorient ourselves with names and pleasantries before the bingo competition took place.

"Hey, Arnie, this is that one chick I was telling you about, the one with manners!" Sexy Mike yelled across the table (my nickname for him... I guess they were not the only ones observing others).

Arnie looked up and we made eye contact as he said, "Oh yeah! The salt lady!"

I laughed and said, "What are you guys talking about?"

"You pinch your salt. So, we figured you must be a fancy type of person!"

I laughed even harder. "I cannot see the salt and I am not ready to start wearing glasses! "

At this point, everyone was laughing, and all the ones closer to over forty shook their heads. "Oh, for sure," they agreed.

The ones closer to twenty just looked at all of us as ancient beings. Of course, I didn't mind. I was young once, too.

"B-24!" The bingo competition started and I knew I was among friends, some I still am in contact with today, and probably all who, if I called today, would recall that story and laugh. I am so glad I went to Bingo that day. I have no idea if I won anything or if I just played, laughed, and healed in the warm embrace of healthy camaraderie and sober Bingo.

A Letter to a Killer

Dear Tim,

I don't want to call you by your proper name because I think you went by that name. I am purposely saying Tim instead of Timothy because I want to grate your nerves. Do I think you will ever read this? No, of course not. You are dead, and not in the 'you are dead to me' dead. No, I mean, six-feet under, dead. Because you were given a death sentence.

Were you once a kind person? Were you someone that a young girl or boy once wished to kiss? I know you joined the Army; you were not drafted. So why did you? Were you that different from me? Did you care?

There were so many 'wrong' things the American government participated in that we had both lived through. Why did Waco get under your skin so much that you made the decision to blow up a federal building with American citizens, including those precious children inside?

It could not have been a quick decision, I would think. I have no idea though. I mean, have I ever been annoyed or disappointed by the actions of our government? Yes, of course, but I never had the thought of causing such harm to so many. I mean, seriously.

Why didn't you just go to school to become a lawyer and go to work to change legislation or flash a few quick smiles and get yourself elected—even in a small Kansas town, horizon stretching out seemingly forever?

You could have made a difference without murder, without changing so many lives, including mine.

I know this is a moot point, but maybe it will do something. Maybe at the very least, it will help me. Maybe it will answer why my life had to change, why I had to fall into addiction and cause my parents, siblings, nephews, nieces, and the many people I love now so much pain? Why did we all have to face the words 'meth addict' as part of our vocabulary and reality?

Like I said, are you ever going to see this? No, I already covered this, but you know who will? People who know what you did. People who know the coward you and your friend were, how you both scampered away like tiny little mice afraid of being caught, but then to be caught by something so trivial. I am quite sure you knew that car you jacked had a missing tag. I mean, the precision and accuracy of the weight of components for your bomb were spot on so do you really want me to believe you just messed up your getaway plan. Were you the martyr? Well, no one sees you as such.

I know one thing is different between you and me. I would not wish ill will on you or your soul.

Kind Regards,

Jennifer Mangini, RN

ADDITIONALLY

S itting in the back of a police car, I knew my life as an RN was over, and I gave up. I knew my life would never be the same and it was all because I fucked it up.

When Sally had her baby and I saw nurses with scrubs, yearned to be a nurse again; it was anguish to my heart. Would I ever put scrubs on as an RN again?

Spoiler alert: Wait, no, this is the end of my book, so I will just remind you that YES I am a licensed RN and that all the hard work was so worth it.

Jennifer (probably age 9 or so)

Author's Note

I am so thankful that you have taken an interest in my book! Let me tell you something upfront, this is my story of how this terrible event changed my life. This is not a political statement or a story about anyone else whose lives were changed or lost. I personally have known a few people who escaped the Alfred P. Murrah building on April 19,1995, but their story is not mine to tell. I have written from the heart and with the intent to, yes, tell my story, but the end goal is to be transparent and show that recovery and a beautiful life are always possible. If you are in need of help, please reach out to your community resources.

I would love to hear from you directly—your voices, your reflections, your questions, so I can understand the ways my story might connect or resonate with your own journey. Also, please leave a review on Amazon or whichever platform you purchased this book from, as your feedback helps other potential readers discover stories that support lasting recovery. Follow me on Instagram: https://www.instagram.com/themangini13.

Acknowledgements

First, I do want to say something to Laurie, my wonderful and beautiful spouse who helps me laugh at something silly every day, who makes the best lunches, sandwiches, and enchiladas ever! You and I figured what living and working in recovery really is. You are always there, and I love you more than words can express. I knew when you walked around the corner in Menlo Park that you and I would be married someday. Thank you for believing in me.

So many people influenced my recovery that it is hard to pinpoint each one's impact. I imagine a very different outcome if even one person had been absent, and writing this book has reminded me how their small gestures shaped my journey forward, changing my perspective forever. A wave of gratitude washes over me as I recall whose laughter, whose advice, or whose embrace provided strength on days when hope felt distant. That said, it feels impossible to mention them all.

A special thanks to all of my wonderful family (in no particular order): Dad, Kris, Mom, Peter, Tina, Debra, Tasha, Charles, Alyssa, Lydia, Rick,

Julia, Christina, Alan, Andy, Tim, and Ryan (and all their beautiful and adorable families)!

And also, to people who feel like family, or maybe share a bit of DNA (again in no particular order):
Jessica Siewart, Val & Gil Maldonado, Sandy Isganitis, Christal (Stooooopid-er) Preston, Janet and Terry Goff, Amy M. Le, Gia Peterson (my lil g), Jo Jo Nunez (George), and Antony Berry.

Some people who always had a place for me or always had my back:
Priscilla Azcueta, Cindy Grant, Kate Kassab, Everrit Altdoerffer, Heather Vaughan, Lana SpottedHorse, and Utona Ward (Sam).

And lastly, my Lord and Savior to whom I would be nothing without.

About the Author

Who is Jenn Mangini?

U.S. ARMY female veteran, artist, animal lover (especially dogs!), and RN. She is a nature lover, gardener, and beach and water lover from the day she was born.

Born and raised in northern California, now residing in Portland, OR, this awesome Gen Xer grew up on an acreage surrounded by walnut trees and small creeks. This was the time she explored the landscape of tadpoles, pollywogs, and her own imagination. Also, during this period, she experienced love and affection from her adoptive family—the same people who became part of her incredible support system later in life.

Jenn is a 50-year-old (ish) woman who is in a category that most people don't make it—a survivor.

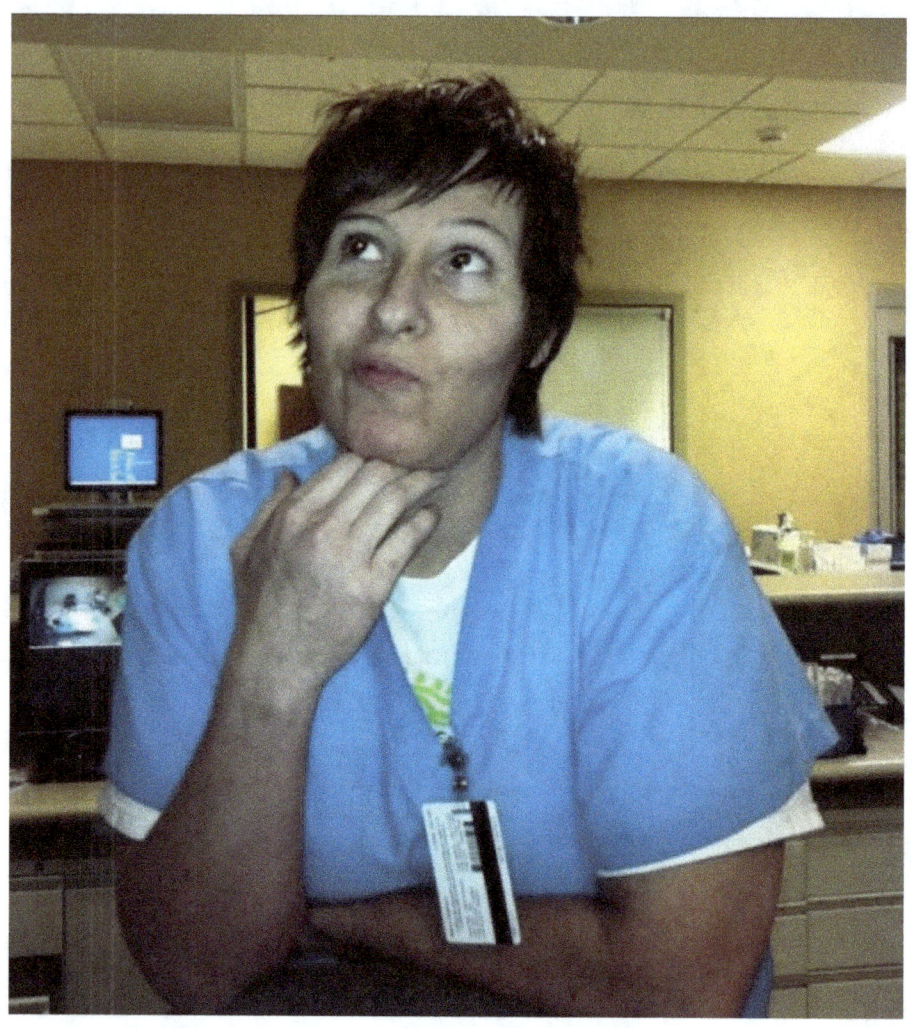

www.ingramcontent.com/pod-product-compliance
Lightning Source LLC
Chambersburg PA
CBHW071153120626
46546CB00006B/2246